As I reflect back upon the 2009 New Orleans Saints' World Championship season, an array of emotions, recollections and vivid details come to mind. Yet, I believe it can best be summed up by one of the words Sean Payton used throughout the season to help motivate the team: **"Special."**

Special, in the fact, from a very early point. When we traveled to Houston in the preseason for a few days of practice with the Texans, a close and united team somehow became even closer. As the early part of the season unfolded, the bond between our players, coaches, staff and our fans seemed to strengthen with each passing win, each passing week. In the blink of an eye we found ourselves on the brink of a perfect season. However, that was not to be, as our team's focus was on the big picture, winning a World Championship.

This special team, this special year not only energized a city, state and region, but it also captivated a nation. Our 2009 season, as special as it was, represented hope, rooted in shear emotion as you will witness in the pages that follow.

On February 7, 2010, as the world watched...this special team, this special year was capped off with a win for the ages. I hope you enjoy reliving the year as told through the lens of our team photographer Michael C. Hebert.

Tom Benson

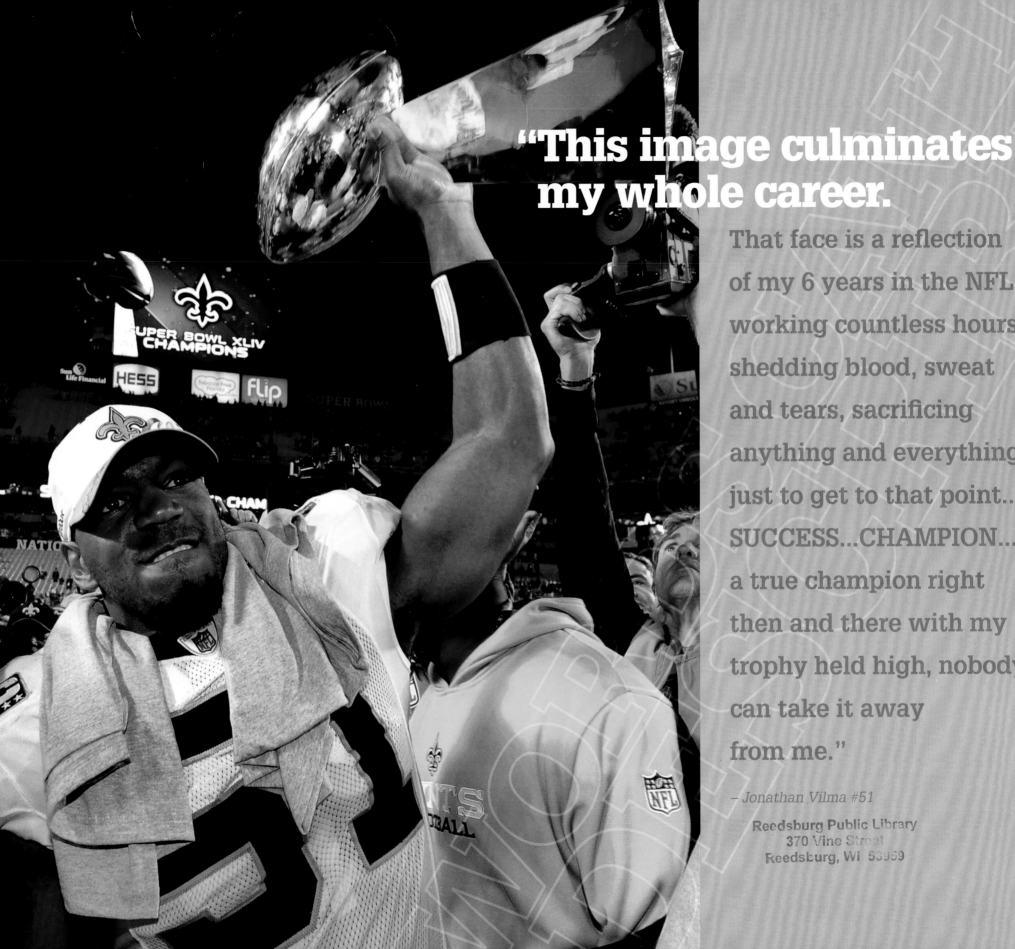

"**This image culminates my whole career.**

That face is a reflection of my 6 years in the NFL working countless hours, shedding blood, sweat and tears, sacrificing anything and everything just to get to that point... SUCCESS...CHAMPION... a true champion right then and there with my trophy held high, nobody can take it away from me."

– Jonathan Vilma #51

"This is the type of play you dream about as a kid.

To have the opportunity to make that play in this game was like a dream come true. This is the play of my LIFE."

– Lance Moore #16

"Players were given Tuesday night off during Super Bowl week,

but the defensive backs decided to do some additional film study that night. The group spent a lot of time discussing their plan to jump a slant route that the Colts liked to use in third down situations. Tracy jumped the route as planned, and returned it for a touchdown. This photograph shows the group on that Tuesday night."

– Michael C. Hebert

"This was my stamp into Saints' history!

Words can't describe how much this means for New Orleans. I am a Louisiana native, and this is real big."

— Tracy Porter #22

"When I was behind Tracy on his way to the end zone, I was thinking it was game-set-match. I knew then the game was at hand."

— Darren Sharper #42

"This is the moment
when we knew the
Saints were going to
be World Champions!
Pierre and Lance both
leaped into the air when
our defense stopped the
Colts on 4th down with
44 seconds left in the
game. This photograph
will be one of my all
time favorites."

– *Michael C. Hebert*

"A lot of rings that we looked at featured the Lombardi Trophy, but our team has such a deep connection to the city, and the fleur-de-lis is not just an emblem of the Saints. It represents the region."

– Mickey Loomis

"I was nervous and excited about the kick at the same time. The biggest kick of my life was going to be the shortest one of my life."

— *Thomas Morstead #6*

" 'That had nothing to do with X's and O's!'

That's what Gregg Williams said to me after I recovered the onside kick. I'll remember that statement forever because it not only defined that play, but also our team as a whole and our passion and desire to win at all cost." — *Chris Reis #39*

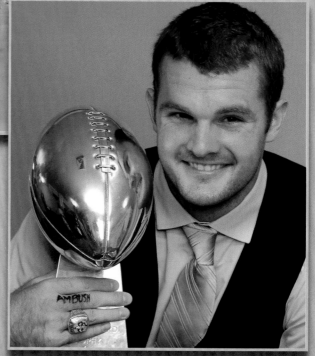

"I told the team during our Sunday morning meeting

that we would be using 'Ambush.' Ambush is the name for our surprise onside kick. I told the special teams unit we weren't going to consider it; we were going to do it. We just had to find the right time." *– Sean Payton*

"Get'em hype. The inspiration

for this chant came from the Marines at Guantanamo

Bay. It goes a little something like this: one...two...

win...for you...three...

four...win....some more...

five...six...win....for

kicks...seven...eight....

win...it's great...nine...

ten...win...again....win...

again...win...again."

– Drew Brees #9

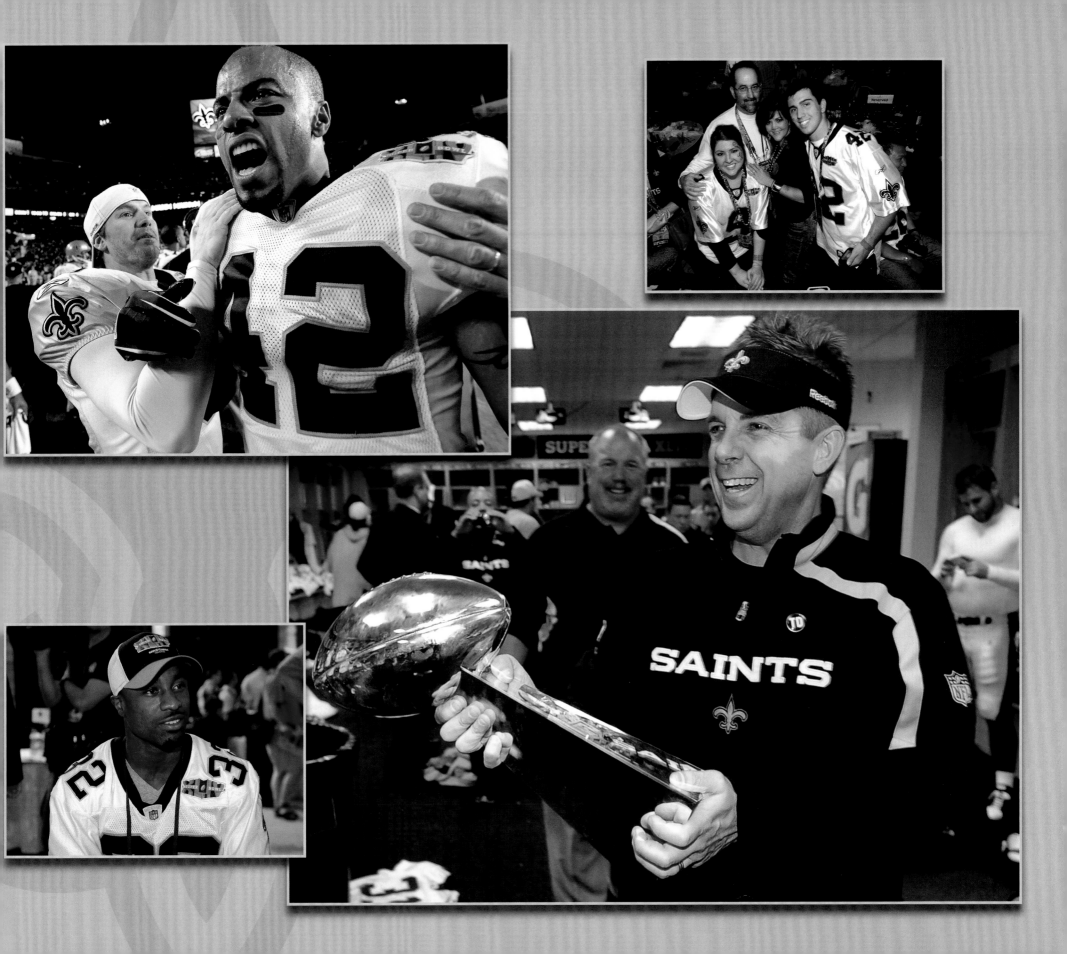

"You don't have to be a Special Team

Player to make Special Plays."

– Robert Meachem #17

"At our postgame Super Bowl party

back at the hotel, country superstar Kenny Chesney plays while Zach Strief and Nick Leckey are not backstage, but onstage. To me, they look like they're in the way."

— Sean Payton

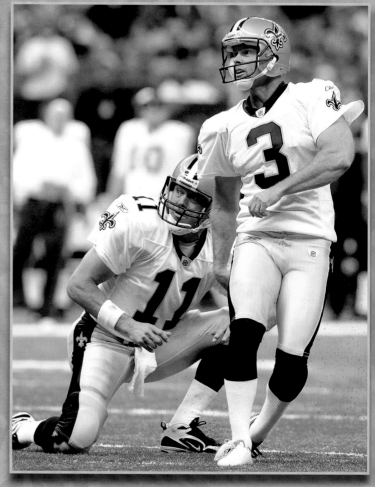

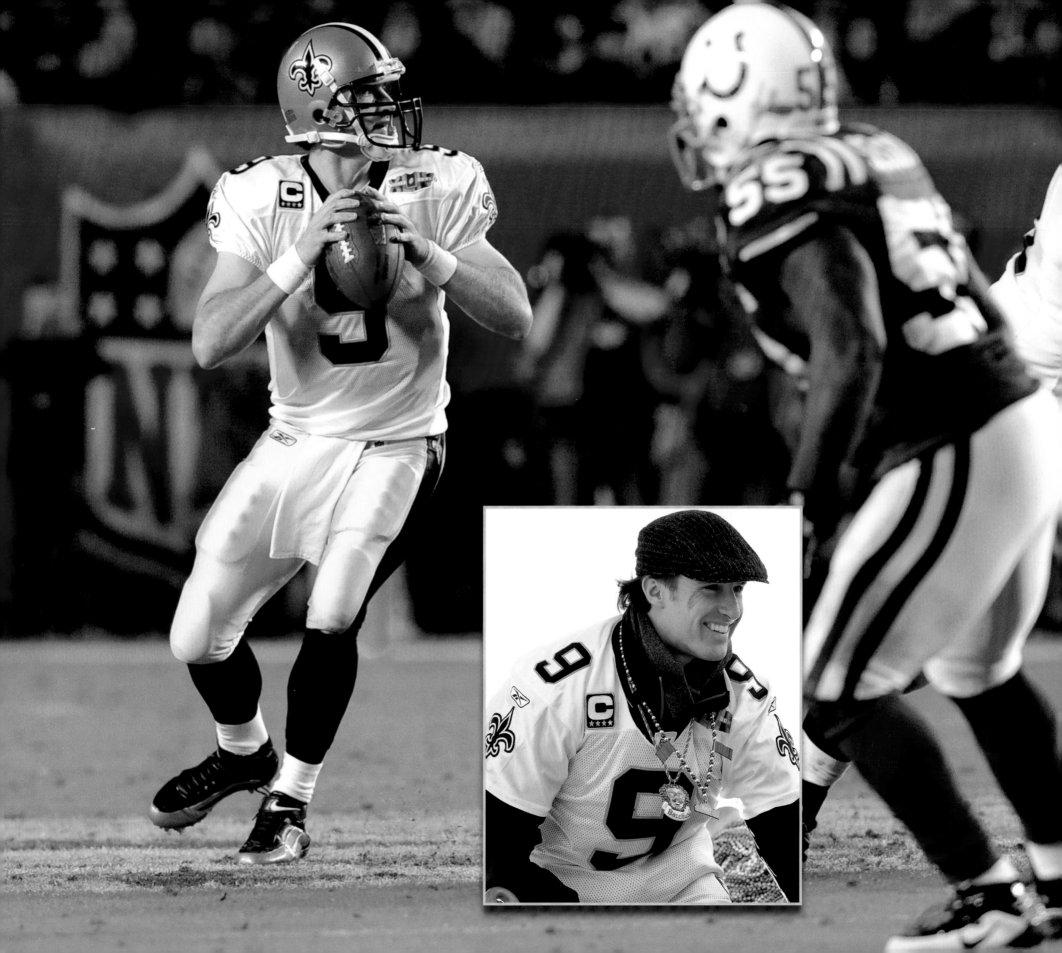

"Ever since you start playing football,

you're dreaming about playing in this game. I dreamed and prayed all day and night about being in the situation I'm in right now and that's what happened."

– Jeremy Shockey #88

"We played for the entire Gulf Coast Region.

We played for the entire Who Dat nation that has been behind us every step of the way. We've been blessed with so much. It's unbelievable."

– Drew Brees #9

"Photography allows us to capture emotion and make it stand still.

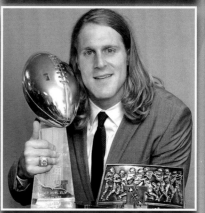

When people look back at their expressions in these portraits, I can only hope it brings back the smile they had the night they received their Super Bowl Rings." — *Michael C. Hebert*

"There was no moment more moving

than the waves upon waves of ecstatic fans at our parade, or the joy of recognizing familiar faces among the thousands gathered. This is New Orleans, this is why we live, work and love in this glorious city. It was an unbelievable experience and my most treasured memory from Super Bowl."

— Rita Benson LeBlanc

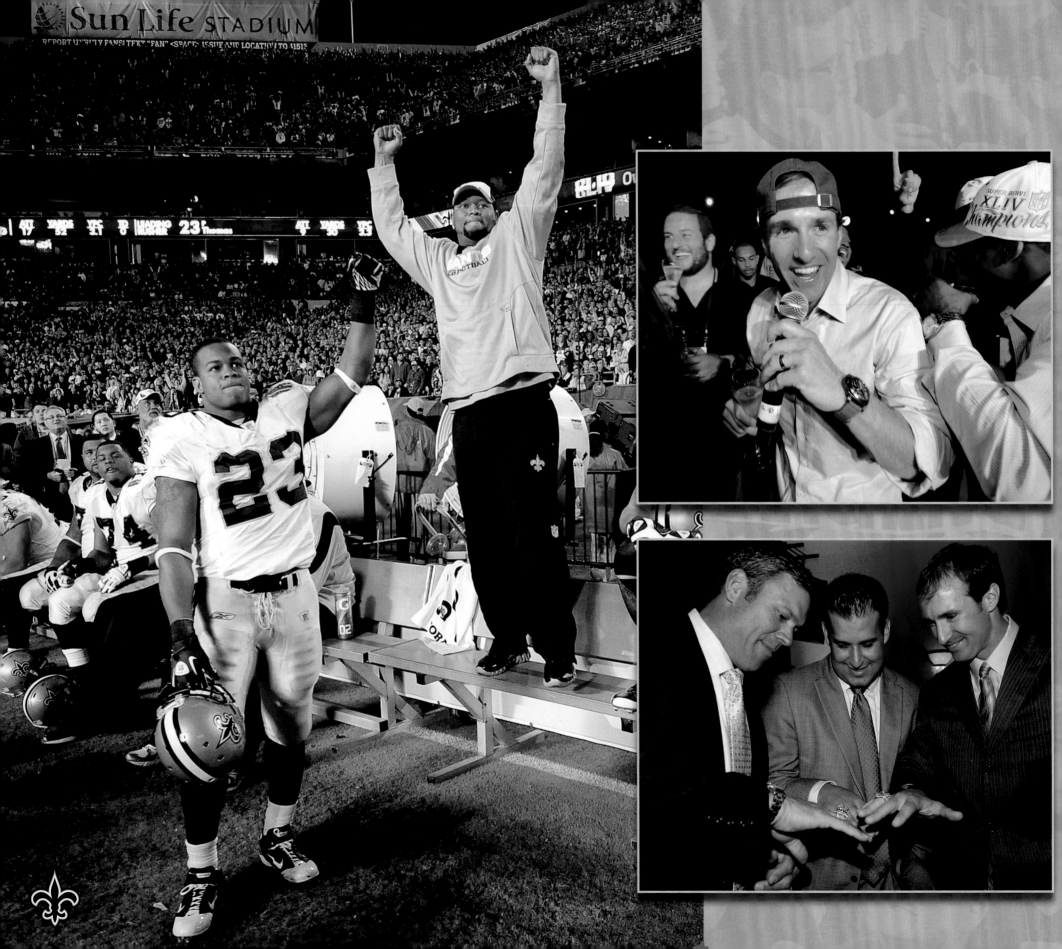

HAPPY LOMBARDI GRAS

"**Like thousands of New Orleanians, Jerry and Janice Romig have been** with the Saints since that very first game in Tulane Stadium in 1967. Since 1969 Dad has been the stadium announcer as his bride sat in the stadium. Their dream came true on Super Bowl Sunday 2010. The 2009 Saints season for my family was one that dreams are made of... beginning with Dad's selection for the Fleur-de-Lis award by the Saints Hall of Fame...the Super Bowl XLIV victory, the Dat Tuesday championship parade... memories that my parents, my brother and sisters and all our children will treasure forever." — *Jay Romig*

HERE WE COME

SUPER
DOME-
NATION

"'Kill the Head and the Body Will Die.' We're not afraid to say this is what our Defense is about." – Gregg Williams

"Our first day in Miami we practiced at the Dolphins' facility. Here posed with Drew Brees and myself are two future Hall of Famers, Head Coach Bill Parcells, now currently the President of the Miami Dolphins and former Seattle Seahawks great, defensive tackle Cortez Kennedy. Pretty good company for Drew and I here."

– Sean Payton

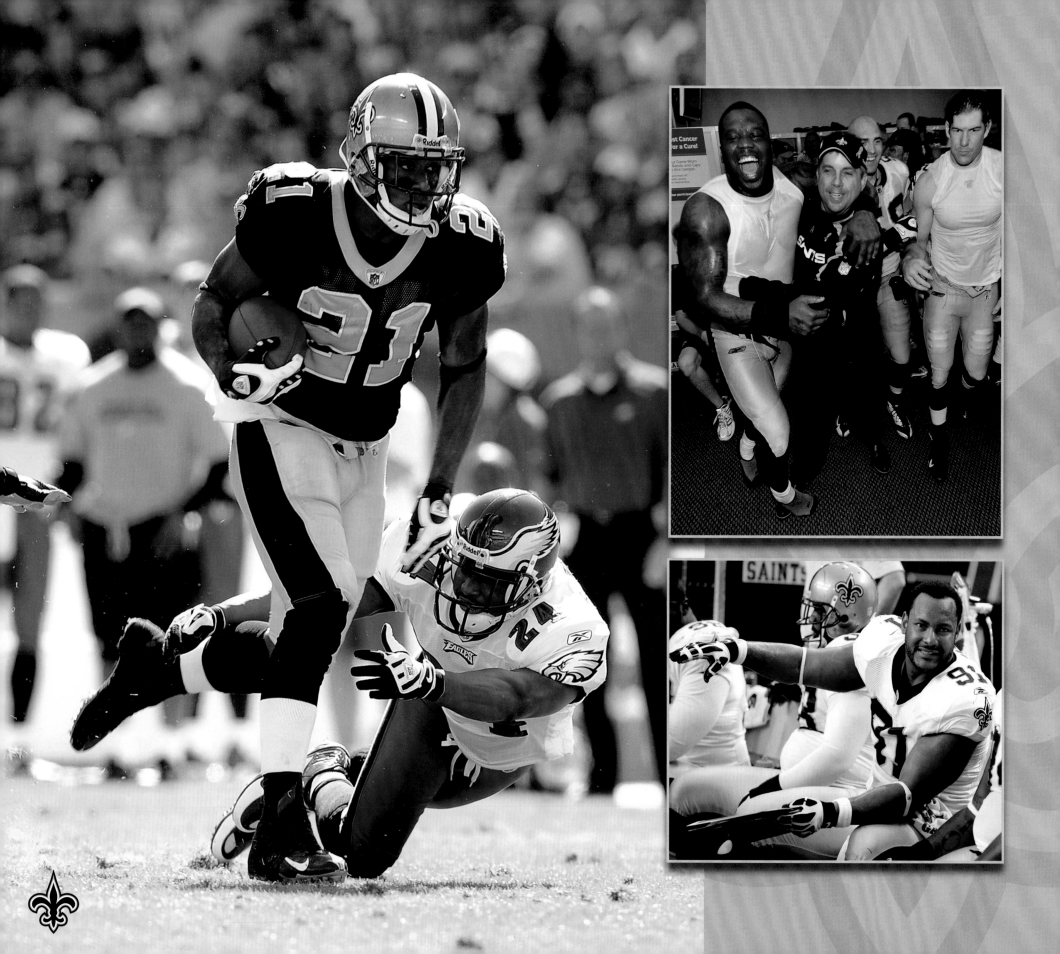

FIRE
EXTINGUISHER
INSIDE

SAINTS

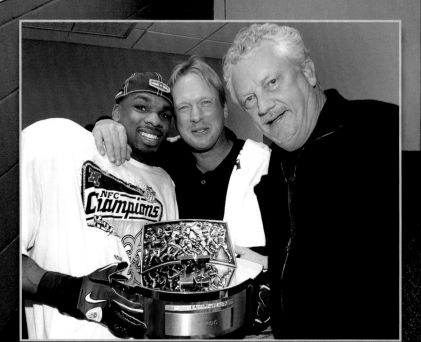

NFC
Champions

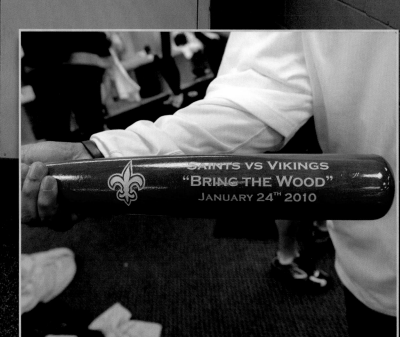

SAINTS VS VIKINGS
"BRING THE WOOD"
JANUARY 24TH 2010

CANADA COOL

LOVES A BREES

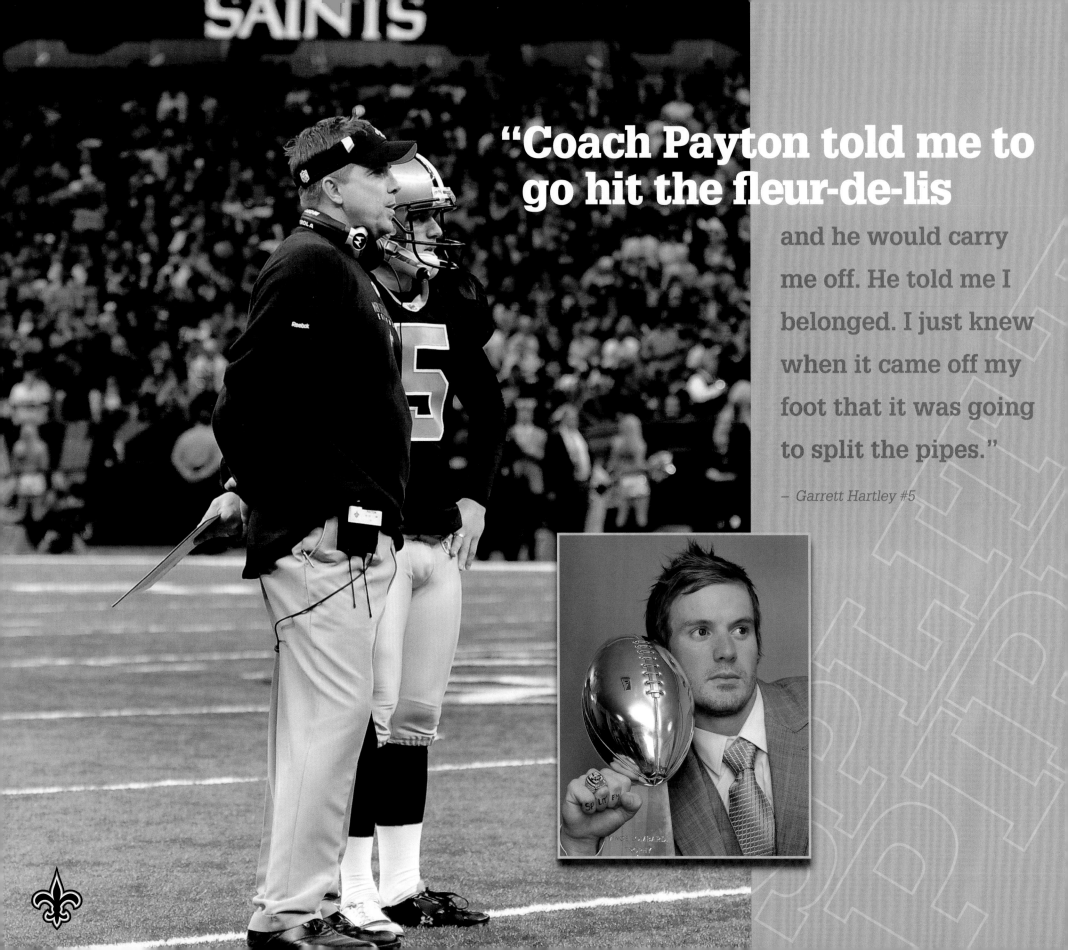

"Coach Payton told me to go hit the fleur-de-lis and he would carry me off. He told me I belonged. I just knew when it came off my foot that it was going to split the pipes."

– Garrett Hartley #5

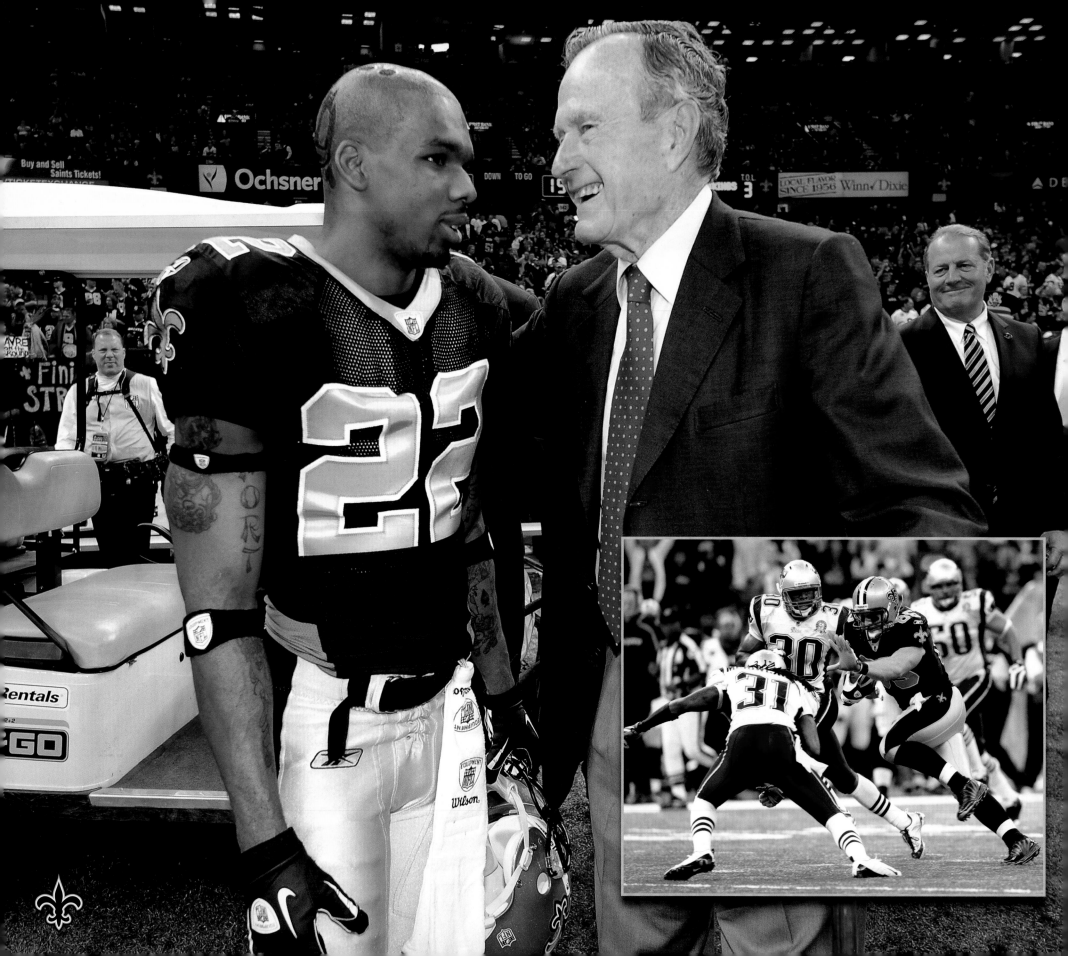

"During times of silence the mind is still at work.

I love the chess match played in silence before the game. This happens to be a photograph prior to the NFC Championship game doing just that. Check Mate!"

– Gregg Williams

"Men are taught that they

are not supposed to cry. Whoever said that didn't
get the honor of leading their teammates onto
the field in the Superdome
in front of the best fans in the
National Football League
like I did. It's OK to cry."

– Deuce McAllister #26

"On a flight to an away game,

Joe Vitt, Gregg Williams and I take a brief moment to listen to some of Joey Imparato's advice for our game plan."

– Sean Payton

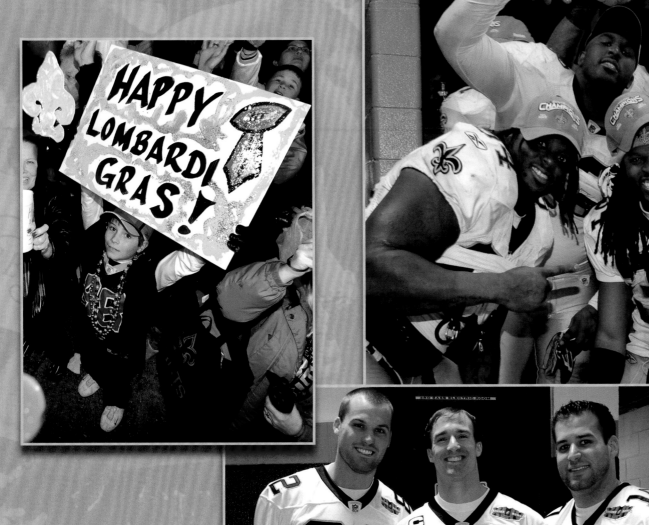

"One of the greatest things

about participating in a Super Bowl is you have a chance to find time to enjoy it with your family. Saturday, prior to the game, the children of our players and coaches came out to test the field and practice with the team. Here's a picture of my son Connor, successfully kicking a field goal. I think he needs another holder."

— Sean Payton

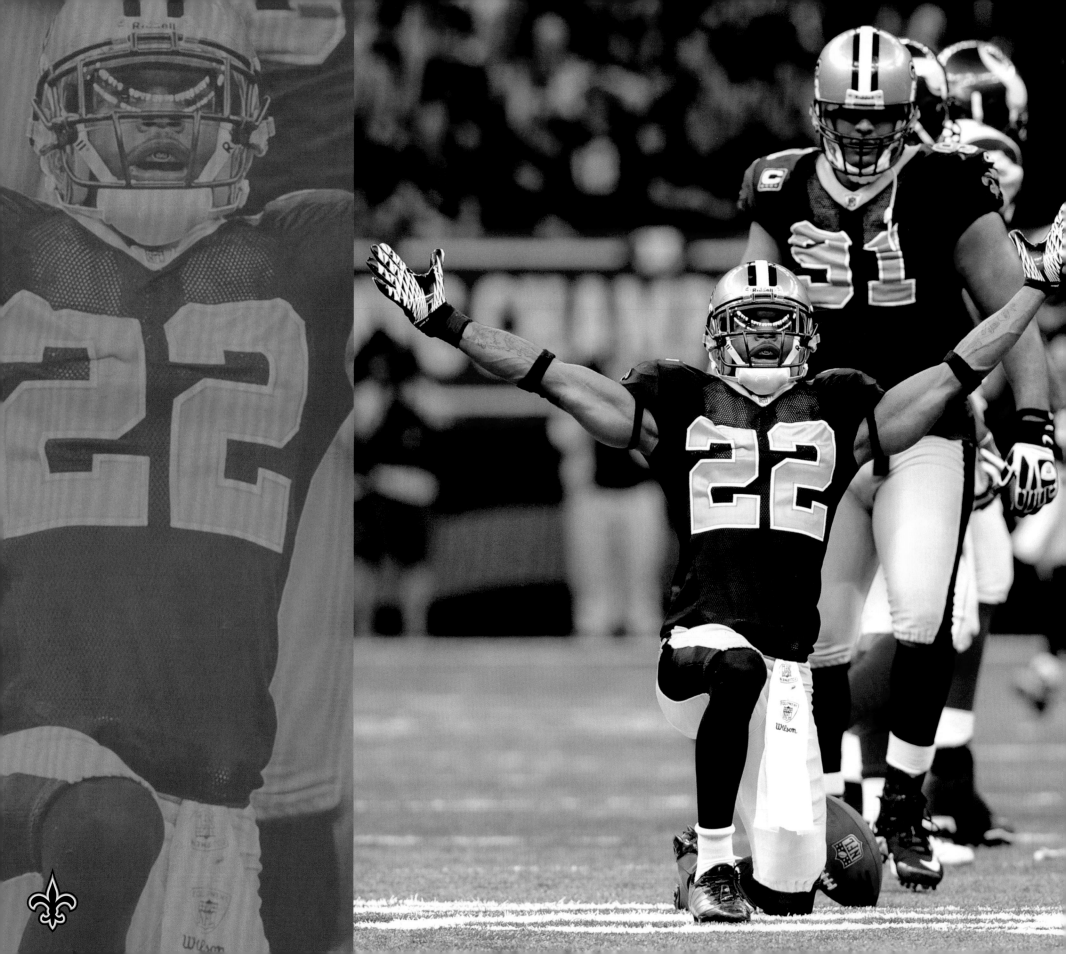

"Answering the challenge! With a little revenge for Sharper at the end." — Tracy Porter #22

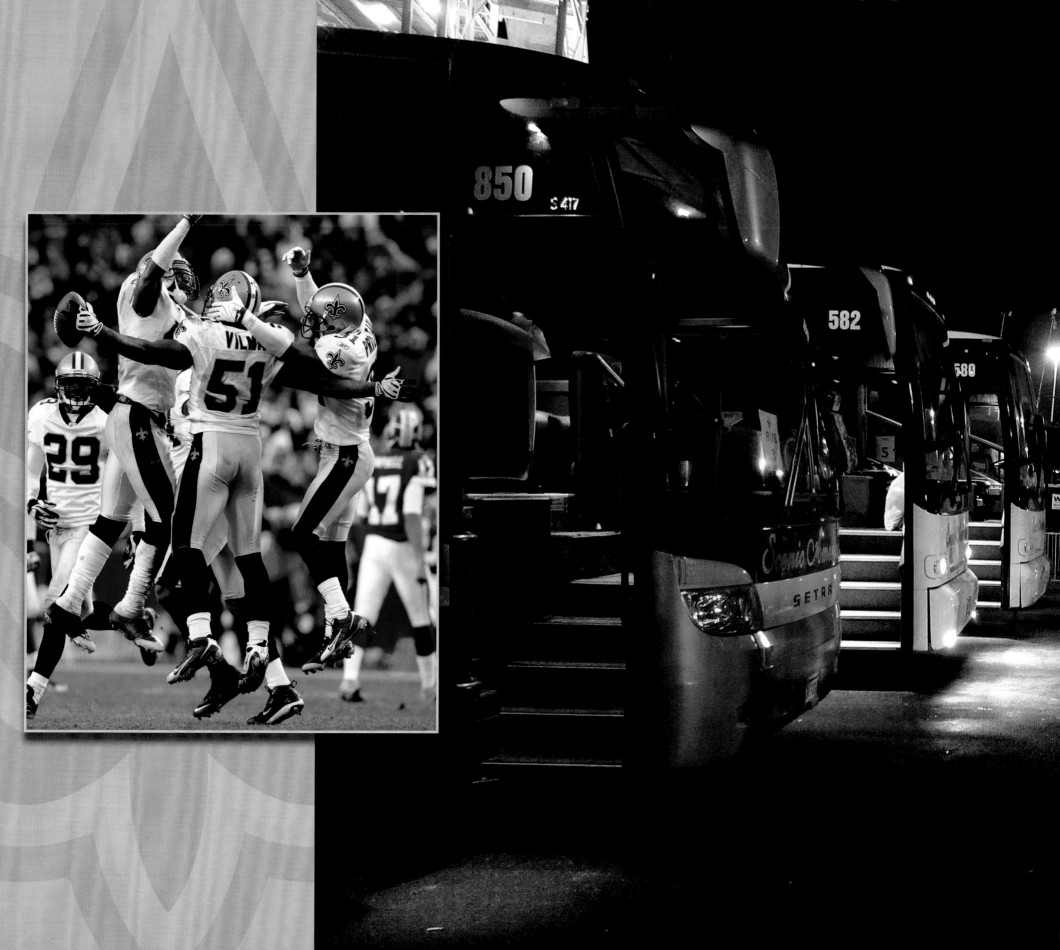

'Gregg is just like Coach Payton.

He's the ultimate motivator and very passionate about everything he does. For him to come to the New Orleans Saints elevated our defense to a level that I don't think any Saints' defense has been at."

— Will Smith #91

'We talked about being the most aggressive team

for 60 minutes. Coach Payton handed out bats that said, 'Bring the Wood.' These are the types of games that you live for." – *Reggie Bush #25*

"The Bottle: Victory celebrations need a gift of bubbly. I told Coach,

my bottle is bigger than yours...and then brought the entire team on stage to open it (the cork broke) and share a massive toast with the crowd. Coach shook the remainder for a bubble spray upon everyone."

– Rita Benson LeBlanc

CHAMPIONS
SUPER BOWL
SAINTS
NEW ORLEANS SAINTS

"You must pay the toll if you carry the ball

against our defense. This is an example of Roman collecting tolls. This is

what we call

a classic

'Whack'."

– Gregg Williams

"The night before each game we show reviews a situation

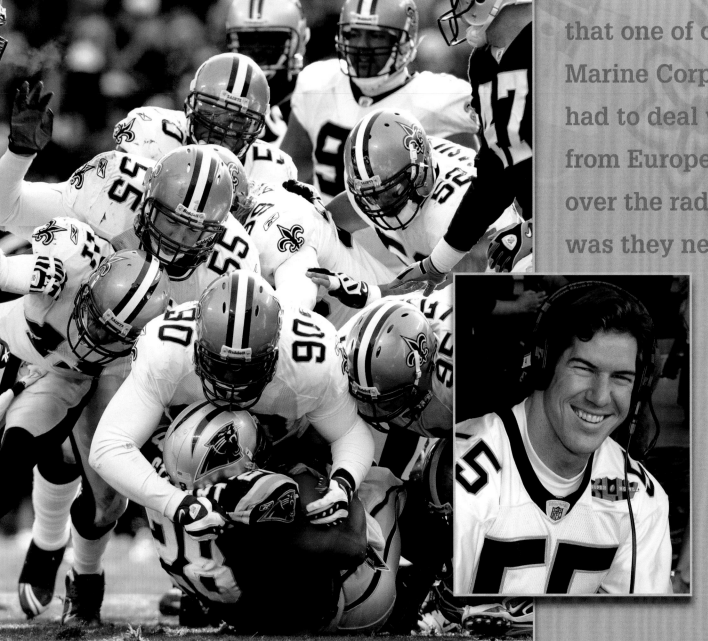

that one of our United States Marine Corp FA-18 Fighter Jets had to deal with during a flight from Europe to Dubai. The call over the radio to the FA-18 was they needed to leave the airspace or an interceptor aircraft would be launched to remove them. The response from

ur defense a slide that

the Marine Corp Fighter Jet
was, 'Send 'em up, I'll wait!'

There was no response on the
other end. Our Defensive
motto is the same.

'We will lock the gate and let
you know when it's time to
leave'.
Come Get Some!"

– Gregg Williams

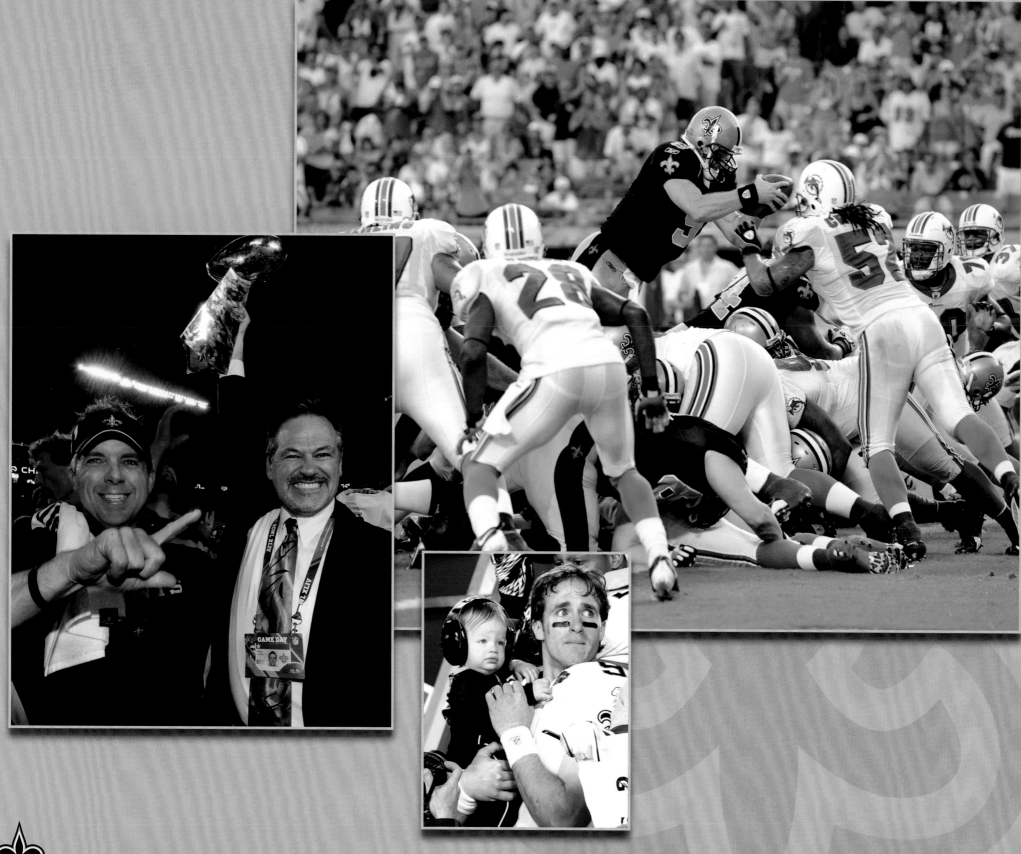

"The Commissioner must remain impartial

but we have come up together in this league, it's our life. Our story would not have been complete without this moment and photo with Roger before the big game. He has been with us from the home opener back in the Dome in 2005 to my Grandfather's 25th year anniversary as owner of the Saints."

– Rita Benson LeBlanc

"THE RING"

The Times-Picayune
WORLD CHAMPS
Saints win Super Bowl XLIV

The Times-Picayune
WORLD CHAMPS
Saints win Super Bowl XLIV

The Times-Picayune
WORLD CHAMPS
Saints win Super Bowl XLIV

AME TIME

SUPER BOWL XLIV CHAMPION

Sunday, February 7, 20

009 NEW ORLEANS SAINTS

aints 31 - Colts 17

XLIV
SUPER BOWL

"We knew they had a great surprise for us. We knew they were getting us rings. We expected them to be nice, but this exceeded expectations."

— Tracy Porter #22

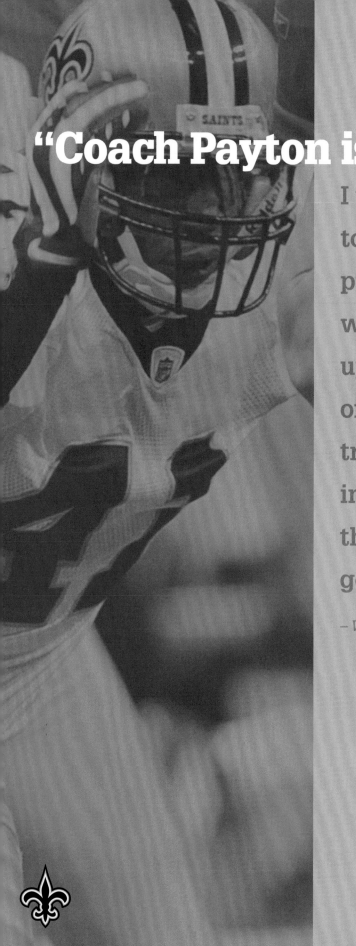

"Coach Payton is not your normal NFL Head Coach."

I think he knows how to relate to the players. He knows how to motivate guys, knows what drives them and knows how to push them to play their best. He does a lot of different things, whether it's with baseball bats or dressing the Pro Bowlers up as bellhops. Some of the stuff is funny, but ultimately a lot of it has a meaning behind it. The players understand the true meaning and the importance, based on the game we were going to play."

– Will Smith #91

"Convention Center Boulevard was the site of some tragic images after Hurricane Katrina.

The highlight of the Victory Parade for our organization was when we rode down that same street four and a half years later; but on this night it was filled with thousands of cheering Saints fans that came out to celebrate with their team. The image in front of Hall C is a reminder of how special that moment was for all of us."

— *Michael C. Hebert*

"This is my first time back to Buffalo

since being the Bills Head Coach. It was special to receive a Game Ball from the team that would become World Champions!"

— Gregg Williams

"This is what we call a 'Remember Me Hit!'" – Gregg Williams

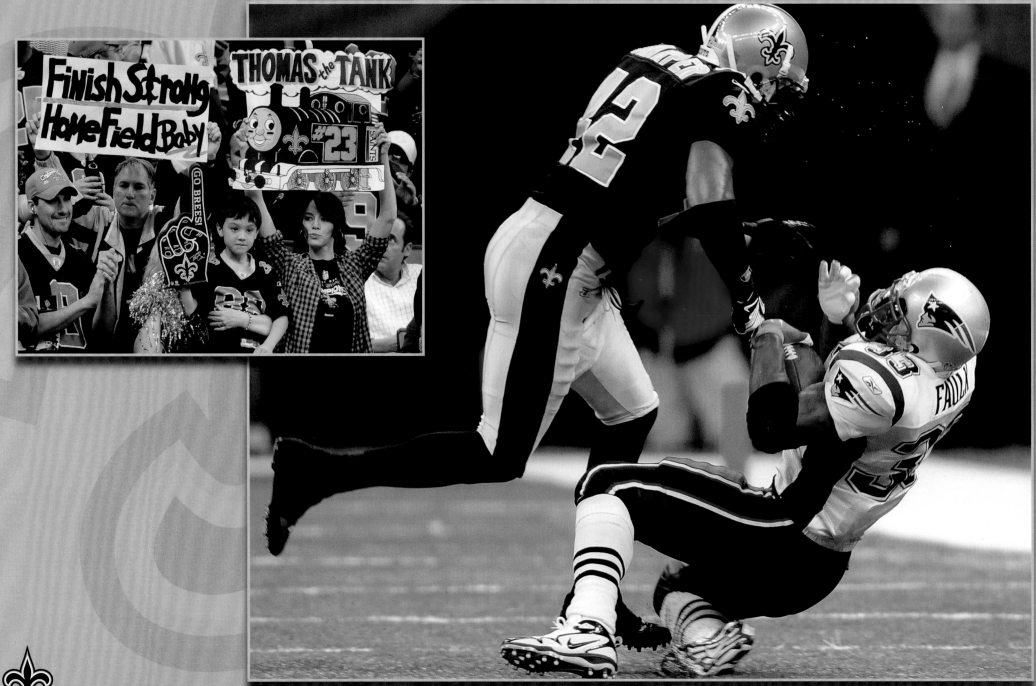

'This is what I have dreamed about

since I was four years old, it's incredible. You can't put it into words. This city and region have been through so much. They have been so supportive this whole time."

– *Marques Colston #12*

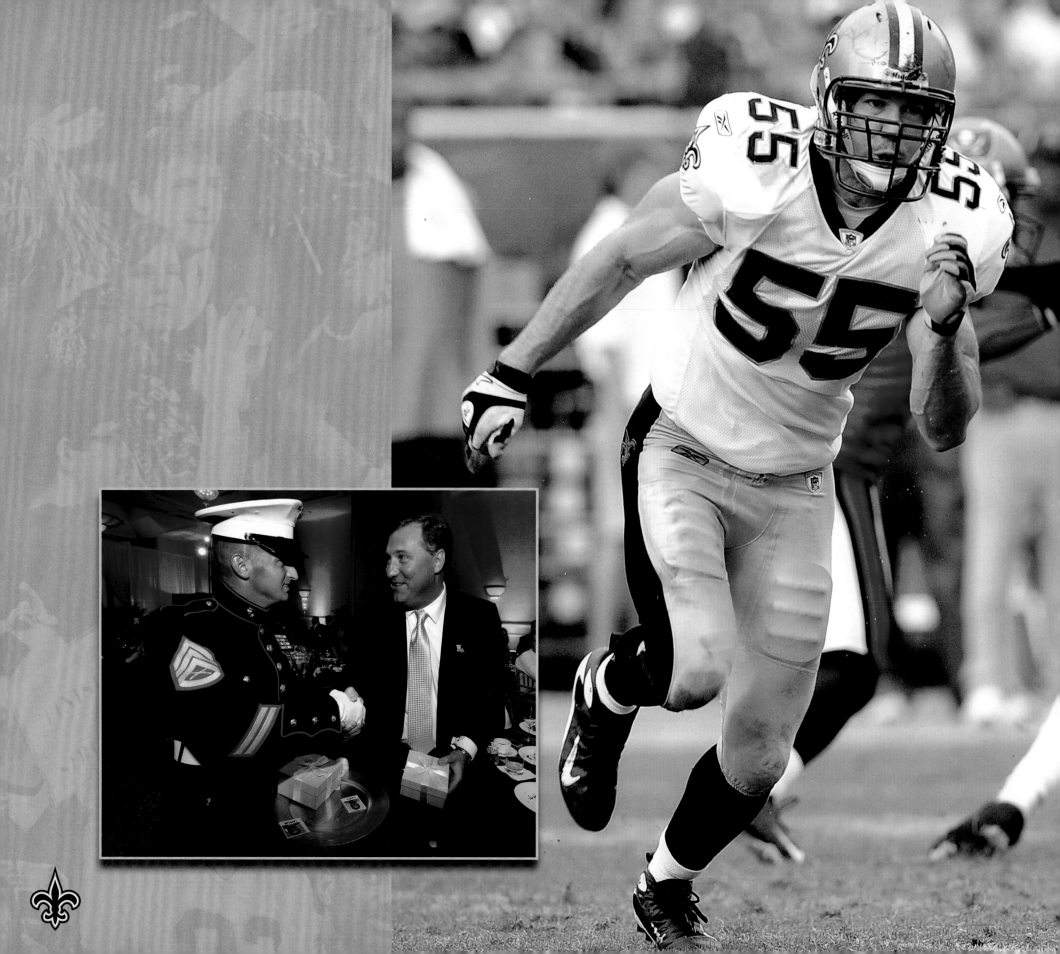

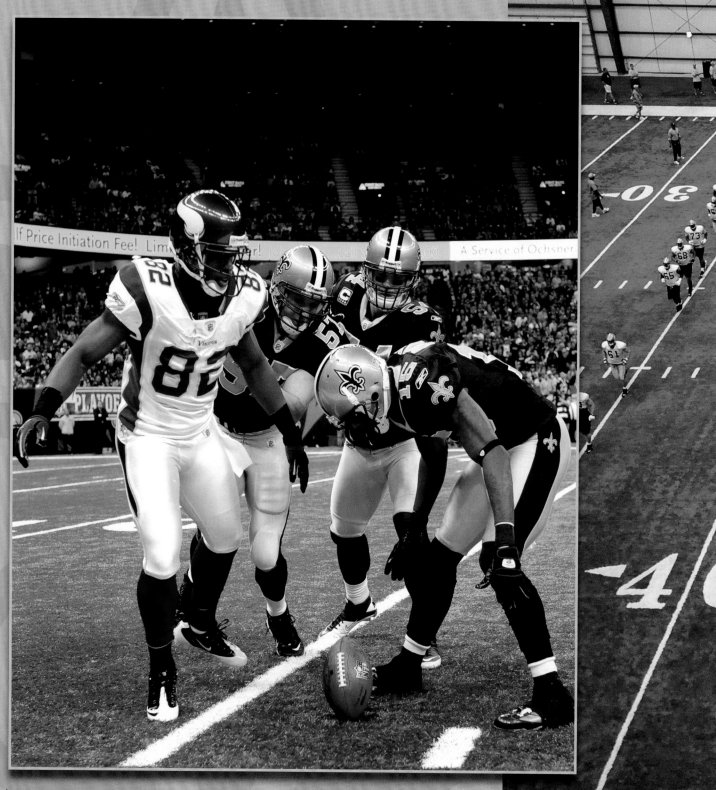
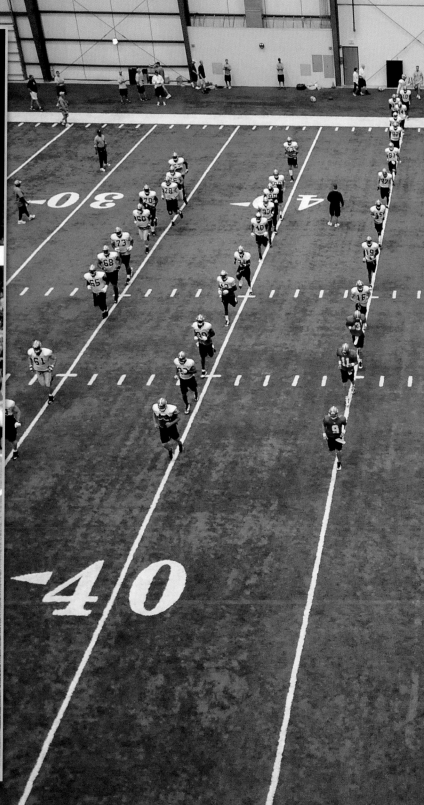

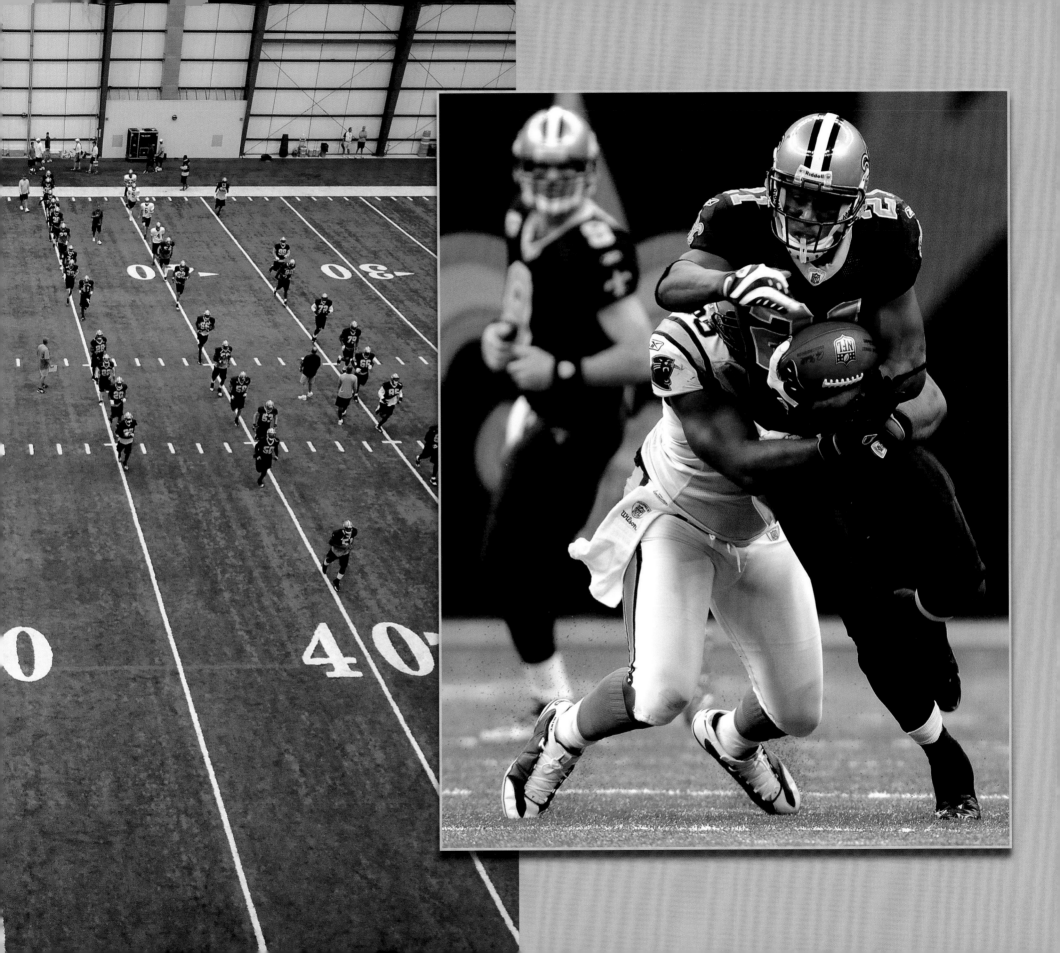

"Taking a break during one of our practices

at the University of Miami, I have a chance to visit with Bill Cowher and gain some words of wisdom. Cowher won his first Super Bowl with the Pittsburgh Steelers against the Seattle Seahawks in 2006. Bill Cowher was also one of the only media members to pick us to win this game."

— Sean Payton

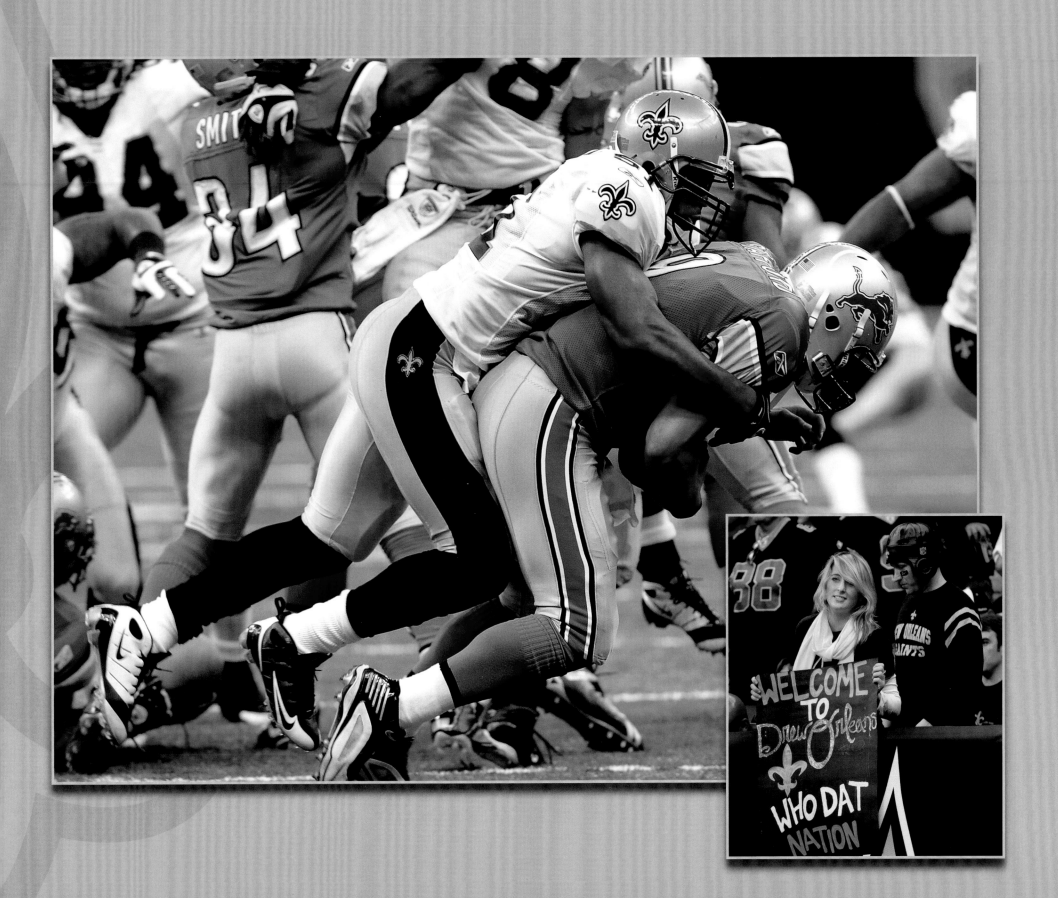

"This is a territorial game and every inch counts, which is why you have to fight every play."

– Scott Shanle #58

"Our organization had a special year

and brought smiles to a lot of faces but no one had as big a smile as Ben Sarrat Jr. and his family. Ben will always be our Jr. Captain."

– Nick Karl

"**In a ballroom behind closed doors prior to the game** at the InterContinental Hotel, Drew Brees and the rest of the offense have a chance to go through part of the game plan in a walk through."

– *Sean Payton*

"**Our offense always walks through the opening plays**

of the game the day before in the hotel. Here we prepare for what we will see and visualize success."

– Drew Brees #9

DREW BREES 9

MARK BRUNELL 11

COACHES/STAFF BLACK GAME W

COACHES GAME BLACK PULLOVERS

COACHES/SUPPORT STAFF CART

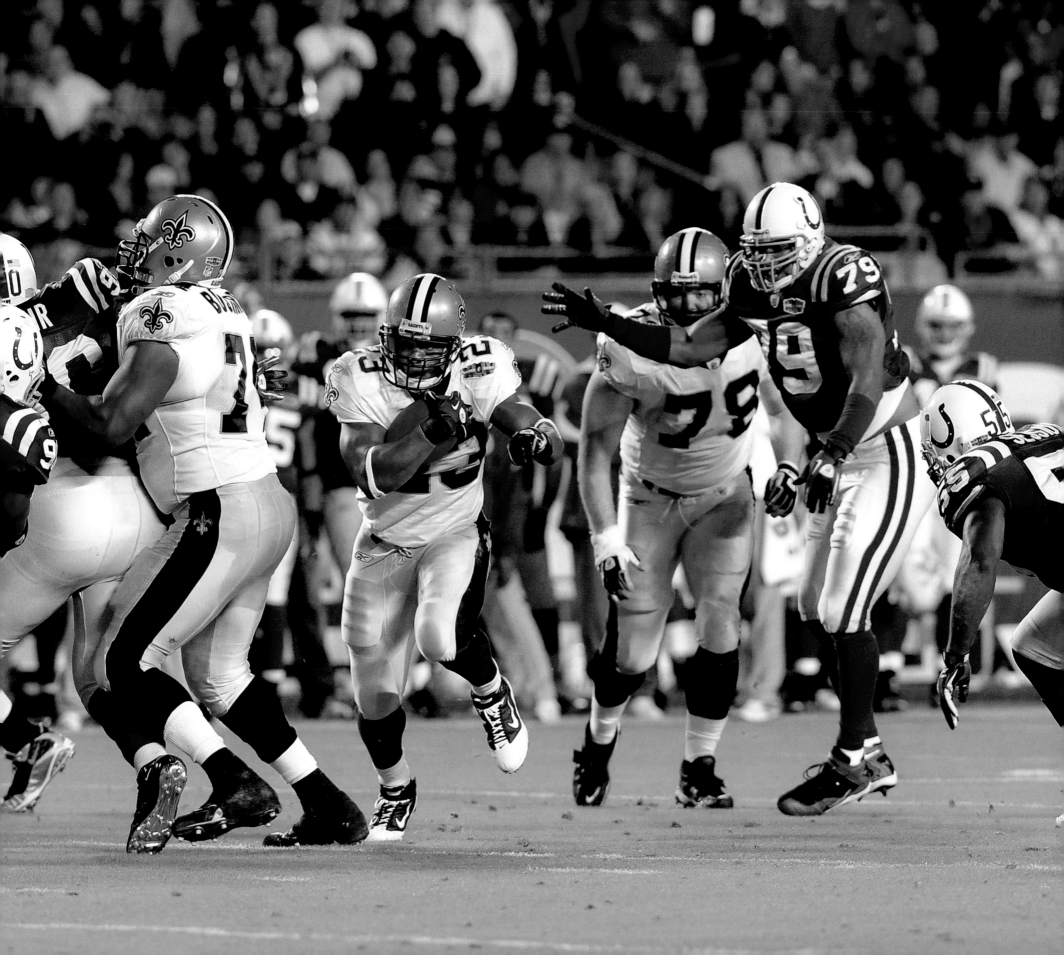

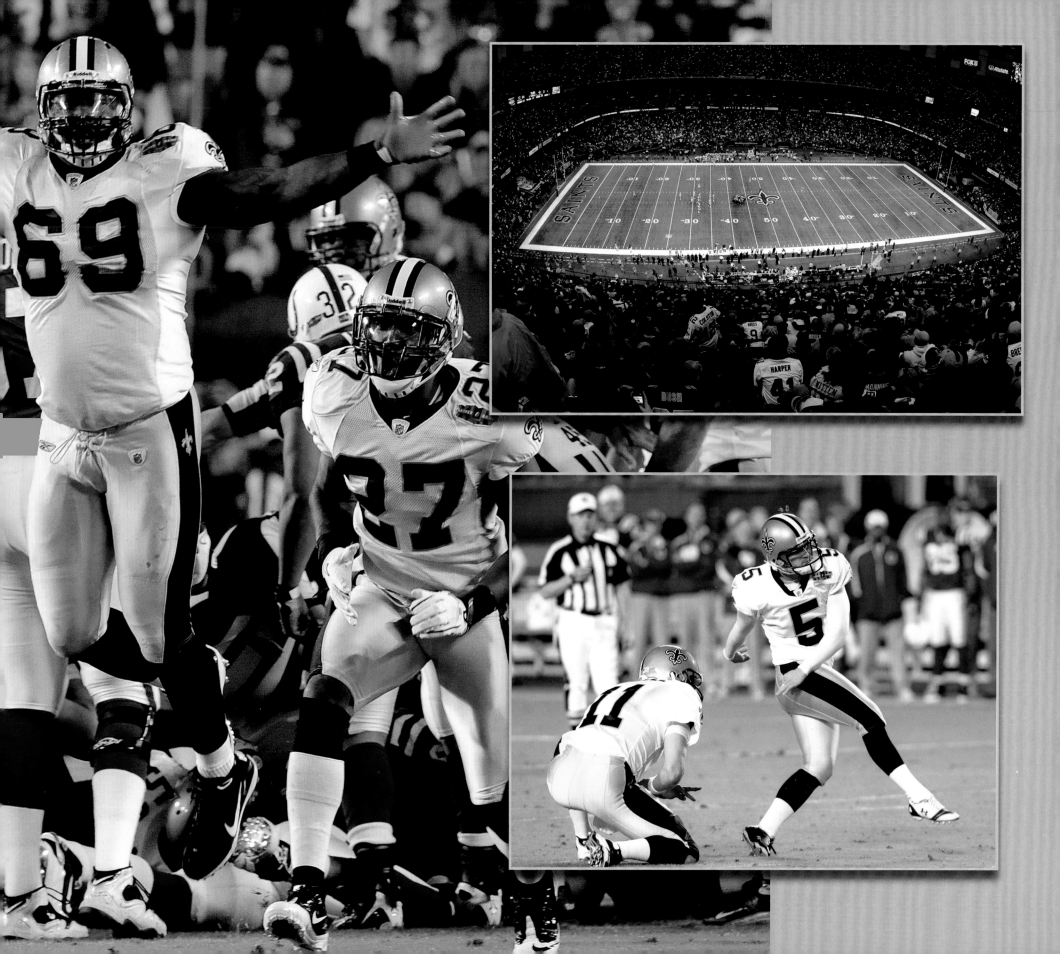

"Shortly after our NFC Championship

victory against the Minnesota Vikings, Jimmy Buffett already has the morning's headlines."

– Sean Payton

The Times-Picayune

SUNDAY, JANUARY 21, 2010   NEW ORLEANS EDITION · 75¢

DEFEAT OF VIKINGS GIVES TEAM
ITS FIRST TRIP TO THE SUPER BOWL

SUPER SAINTS

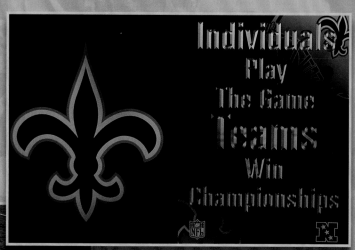

Individuals
Play
The Game
Teams
Win
Championships

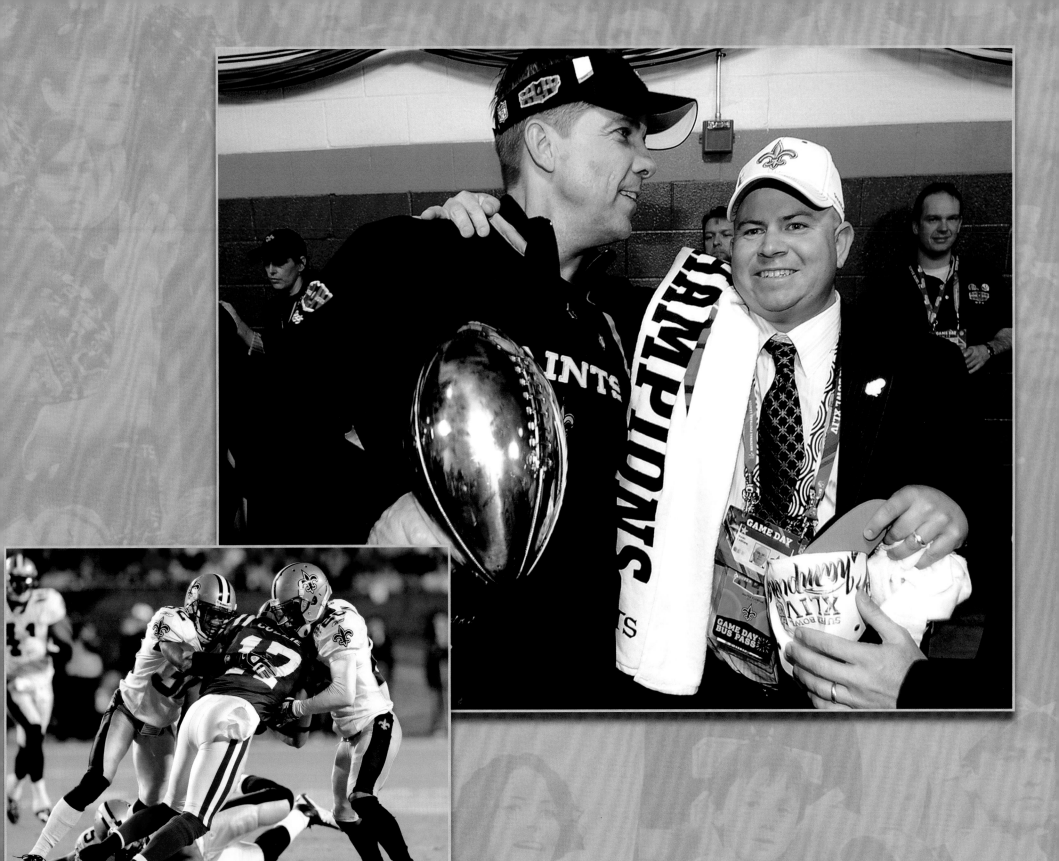

"This group of offensive lineman has proven

themselves as one of the best in the league and is a huge reason for our success. I love these guys...I trust them with my life."

– Drew Brees #9

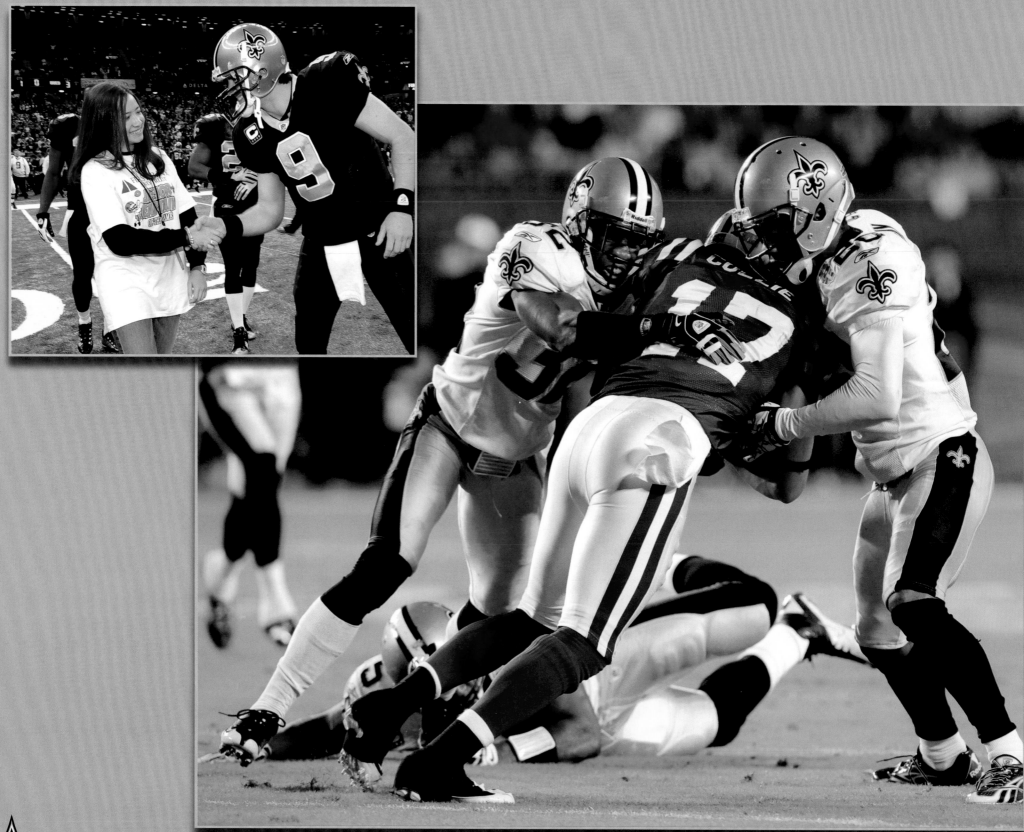

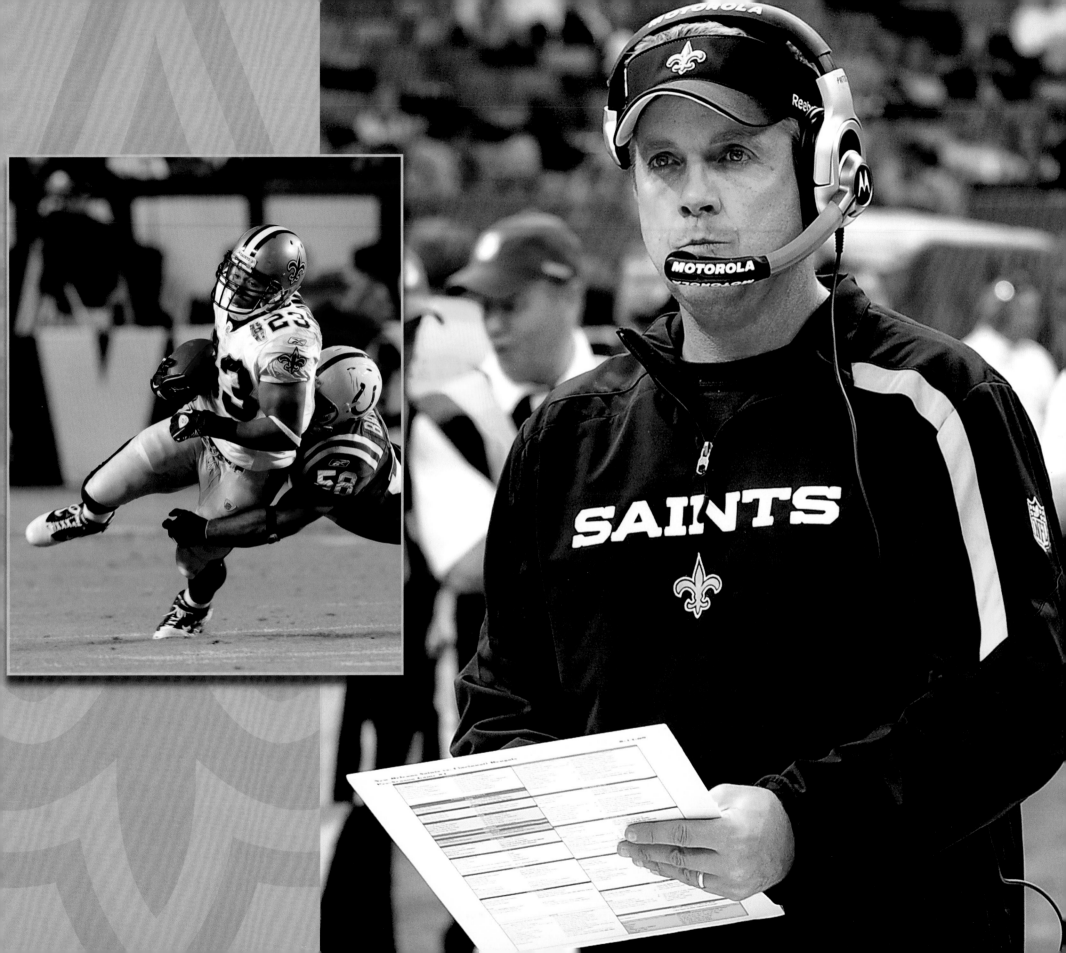

"If you believe in heaven

and you believe Vince

Lombardi is there

looking down on his

grandson, it doesn't

get any better."

– Sean Payton

"The Benson Family and the greater Saints

organization are wonderful supporters of the U.S military. Our men and women in uniform are always welcomed with dignity, respect, and warm hospitality...we are truly honored to count the New Orleans Saints as friends"

– CDR Greg McWherter
Commanding Officer/Flight Leader
U.S. Navy Blue Angels

"Saints' games bring

people together from all walks of life. People help in different ways using their influence to keep NOLA moving forward."

– Rita Benson LeBlanc

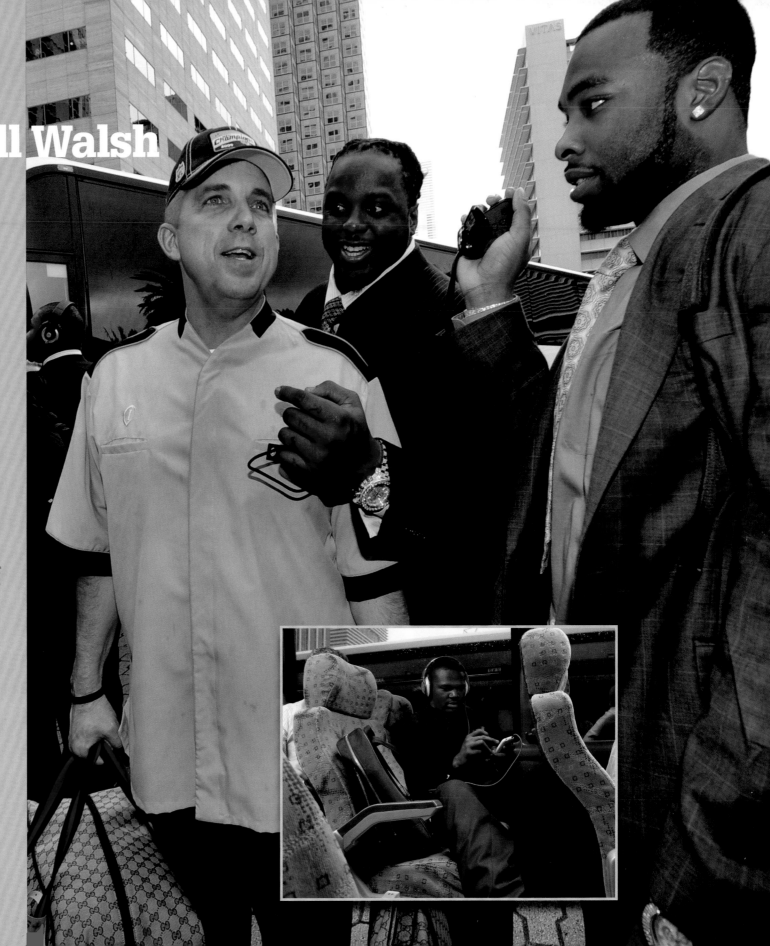

"We stole a Bill Walsh idea and put our own little twist on the bellhop routine. Our Pro Bowl players from left to right, Jon Vilma, Roman Harper, Jahri Evans, Jonathan Goodwin, Jon Stinchcomb, Drew Brees and myself await our team, greet them and try to make some additional tip money."

– Sean Payton

"This is a great example of how much communication

there is on the sideline. Scott Fujita and I are talking about what just happened on the field, while Charles Grant is showing us pictures of what he saw. The best thing about this picture is you see no coaches. They trusted us so much that they let us work out any issues we had on the sideline with each other. That's when you know you have something special."

– Jonathan Vilma #51

"We love playing for our fans who give us the support and motivation to win every Sunday." — Scott Shanle #58

THIS IS NEXT YEAR

HAPPY B-DAY DREW

WE DID!

PROMISED LAND

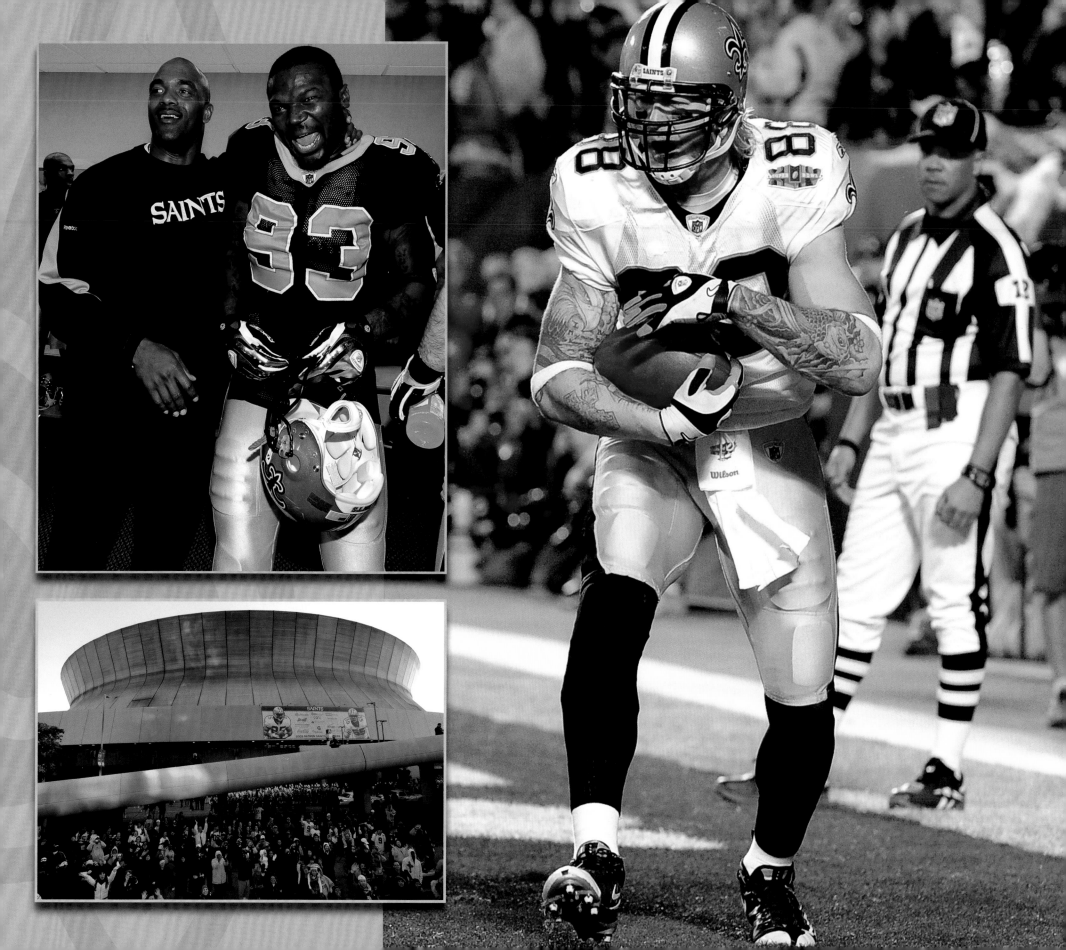

"This is for New Orleans. Everything we did, the city was behind us.

We dedicate this all to the fans. New Orleans probably has the greatest fans in the world. We had to give them something special and we did."

– Pierre Thomas #23

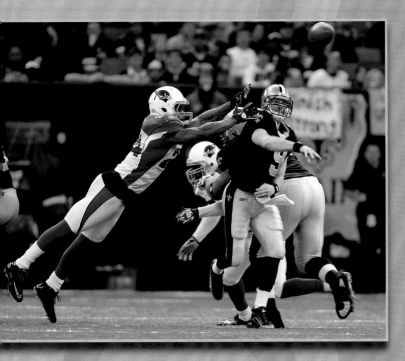

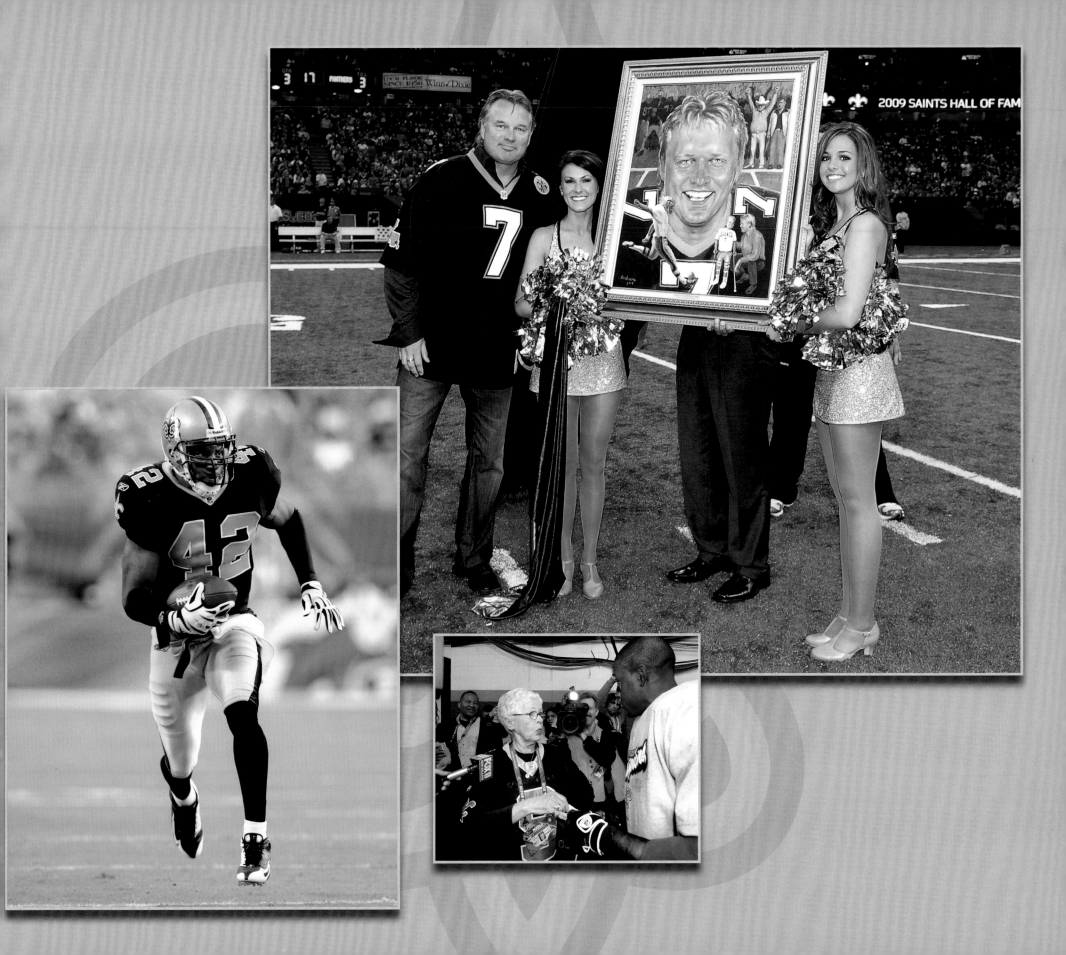

2009 SAINTS HALL OF FAM

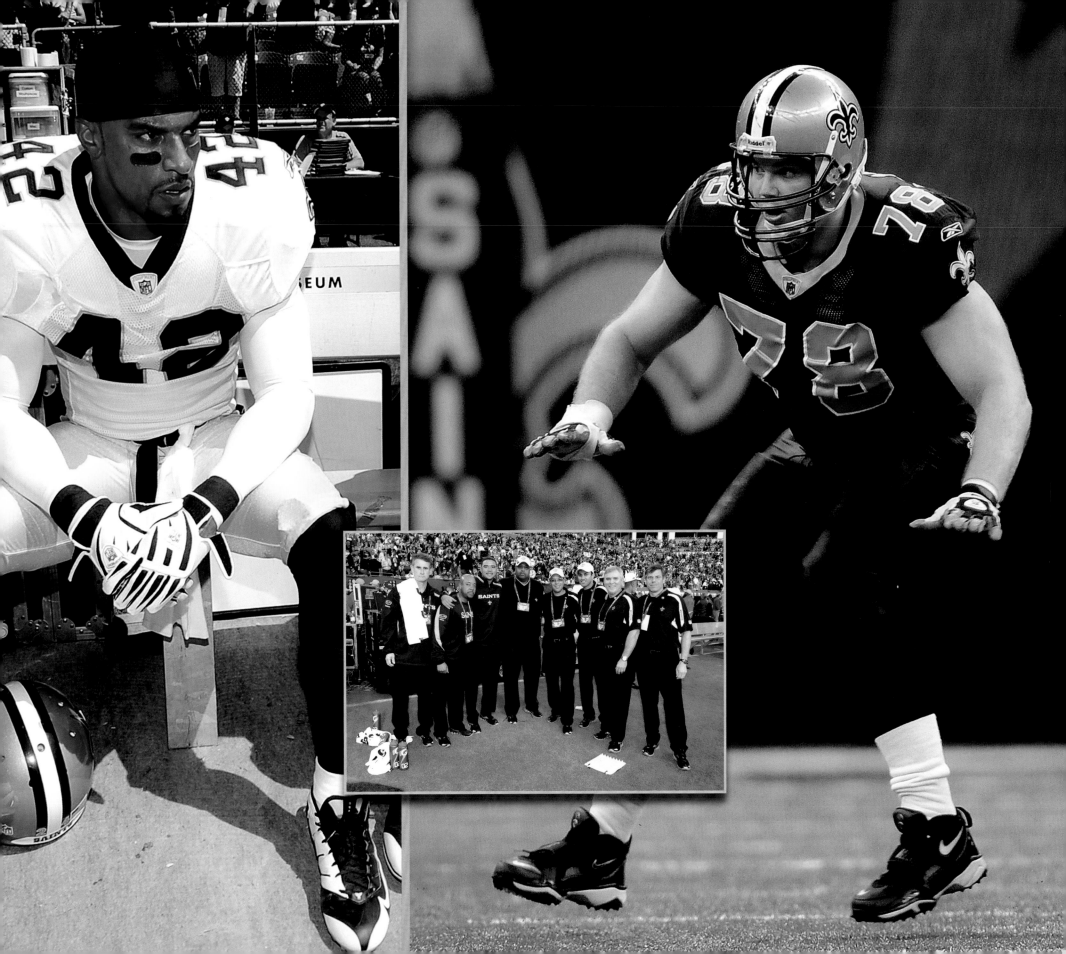

4:38 - Kicker - Snapper - Hol
4:43 - Return Spec.
4:48 - QB's - RB's - TE's - WR's
4:53 - DB's
5:00 - OL - DL - LB's
5:20 - Clear Field
5:32 - 2 Min. Warning
5:44 - Take Field
5:45 - Game Time

"O" Pla

OFFENSIVE PLAYBOOK CART

PUNTER
"TOGETHER" TODAY
"TOGETHER" FOREVER

INTRO TEAM

CAPTAINS
9
51
91
42
54
26

OKS "D"

DEFENSIVE PLAYBOOK CART

"The statement on the dry erase board–
Win Together Today
Walk Together Forever–

wasn't a message to the team for the Super Bowl. It was the message during training camp for the 2009 Season. One day at a time, one game at a time. And in the end, this special group of people that showed great character and determination during the journey will walk together forever as World Champions."

– Coach Joe Vitt

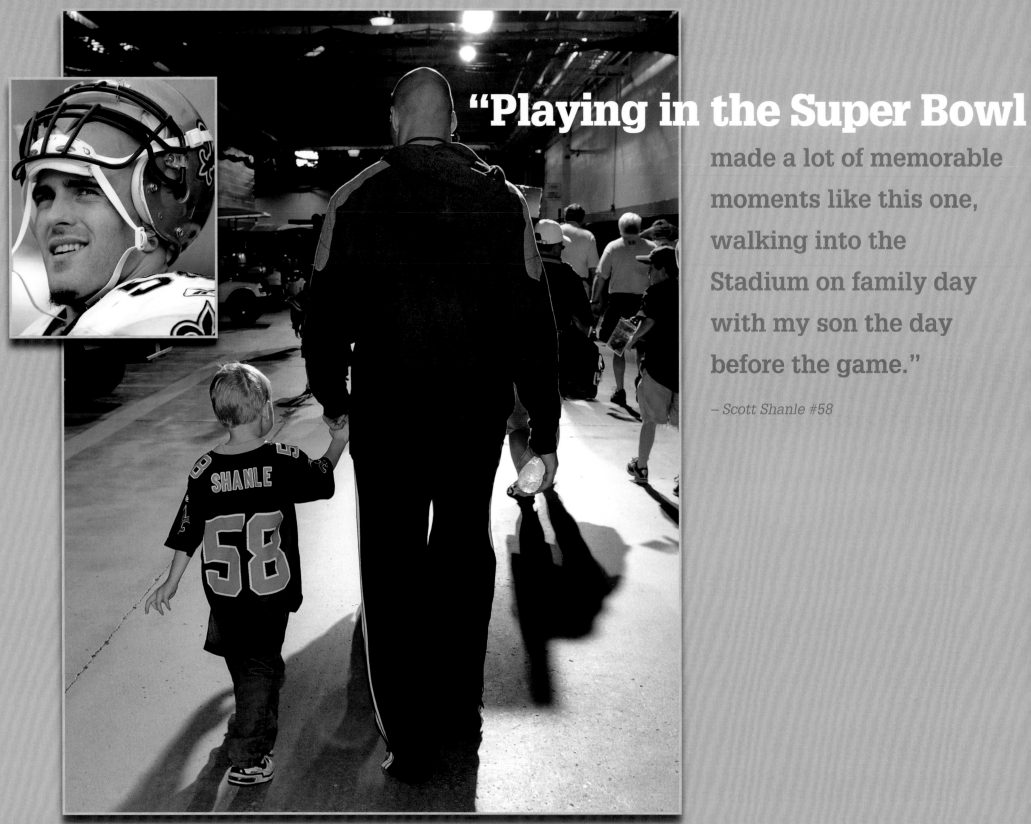

"Playing in the Super Bowl made a lot of memorable moments like this one, walking into the Stadium on family day with my son the day before the game."

— *Scott Shanle #58*

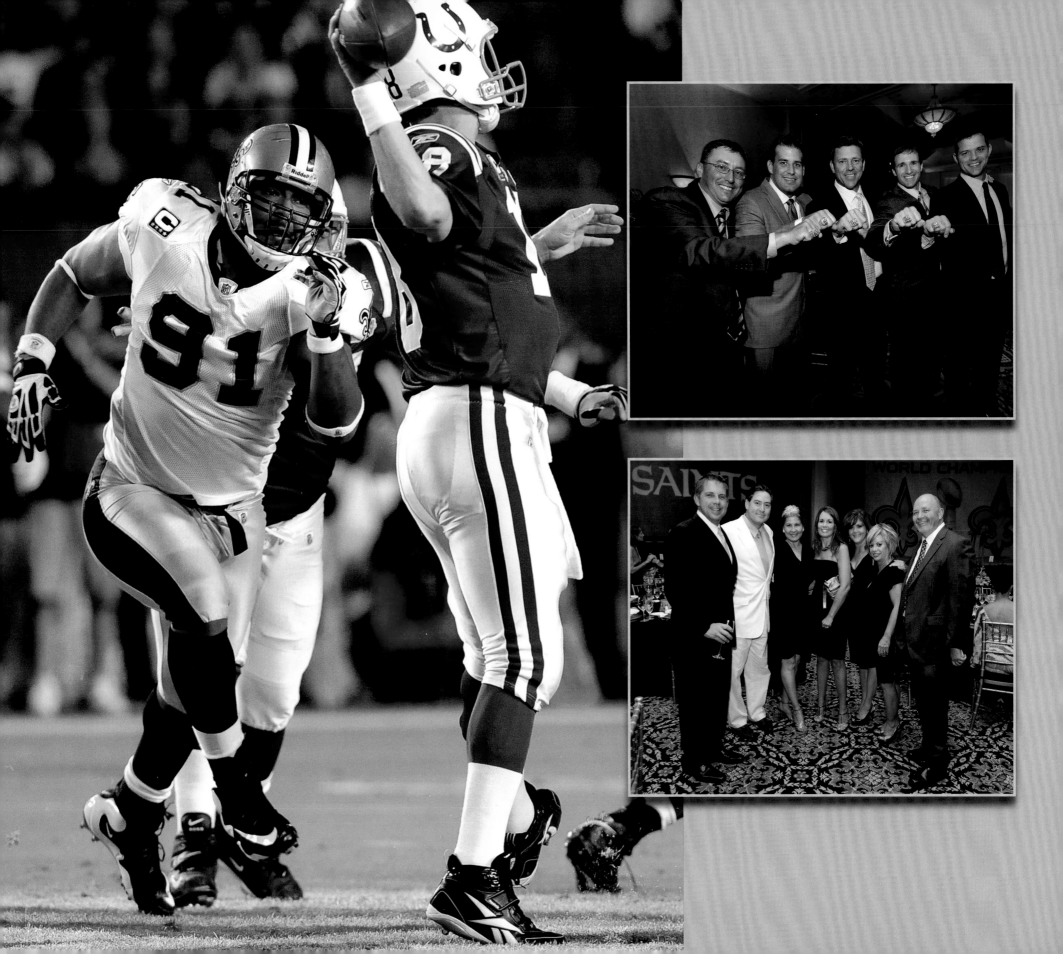

"Two of music's greatest,

Jimmy Buffett and Kenny Chesney, get a unique moment to share in the victory of our NFC Championship Game, posed here with the George Halas Trophy."

– Sean Payton

"Coming on a blitz against Peyton Manning

I knew I couldn't get to him. But the fact that we were able to get pressure on him and at least get a hand in his face and hurry his throws would benefit us in the end."

– Jonathan Vilma #51

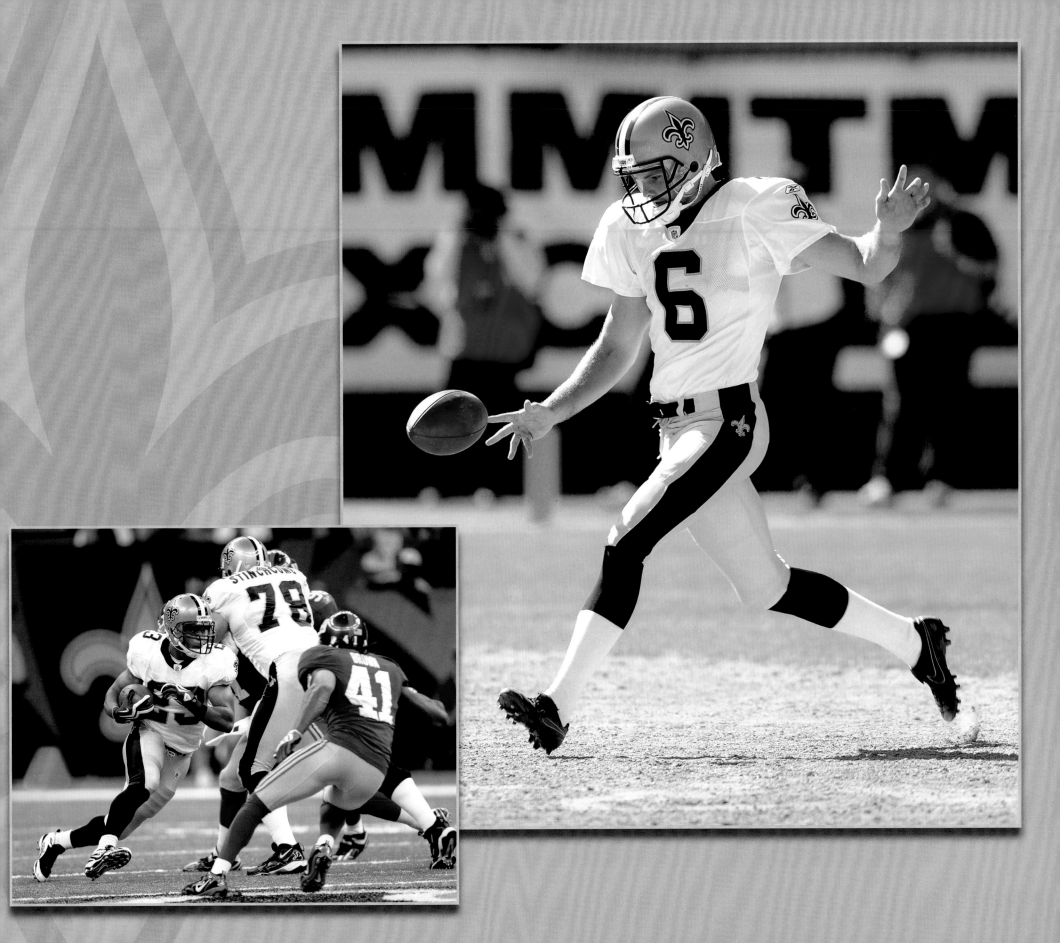

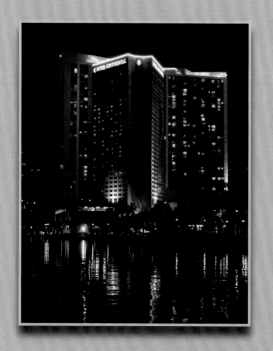

The Times-Picayune

WORLD CHAMPS

Saints win Super Bowl XLIV

Reebok

"BRING IT HOME"

SUPER BOWL XLIV
SAINTS VS COLTS
"BRING THE WOOD"
FEBRUARY 7TH 2010

"During the Giants game I was in the stands at the Superdome as a Saints fan.

My playing days seemed to be behind me and I was on the outside looking in just pulling for my old teammates. And then I got the call. I am going to be playing against the Patriots on Monday Night Football in the Dome. I felt like a Rookie again and just didn't want to let anyone down. Next thing I know the ball comes my way and I make a play. You could say it was my Superbowl."

– *Mike McKenzie #34*

"After practice on Friday at the University of Miami,

Sean said, 'I want all of you to bring your sons to practice at the stadium tomorrow. Let them run out on the field. I want them to have a pick-up game while we're doing our walk through. Let them enjoy this moment with you.' He's one of those guys that is constantly allowing players to bring their kids into the locker room and attend Saturday walk through. Sean likes us to have our families around. During Super Bowl week he wanted the families to be a part the experience as much as it was for us as a team."

– Drew Brees #9

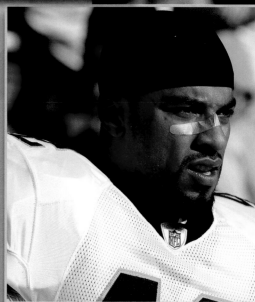

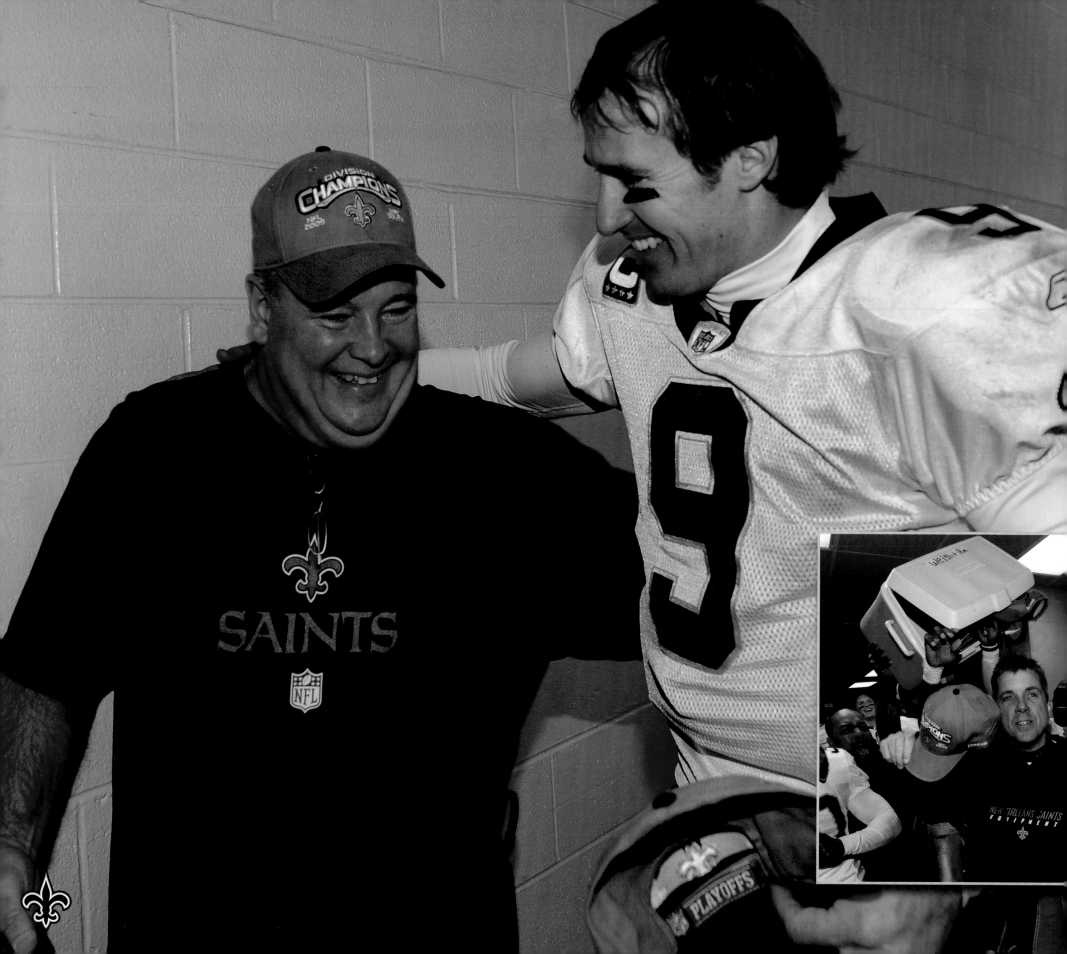

"It's pretty incredible, in fact, I think it's absolutely perfect because nothing was left out on that ring as far as symbols of our season. Things that might not mean anything to somebody else but to us, to our team, every little piece of that ring has a meaning and that's what's important."

– Drew Brees #9

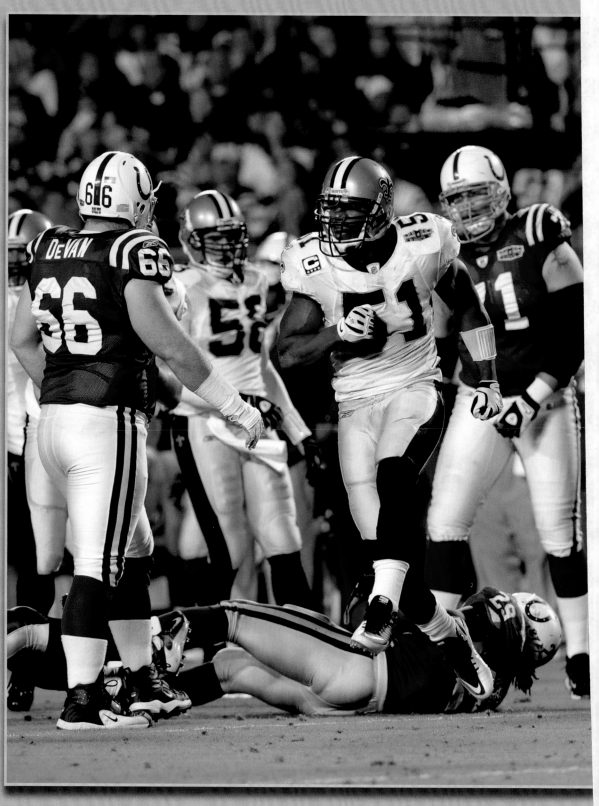

"I often have Saints fans tell me that I have the best job in the world."

As Team Photographer for the World Champion New Orleans Saints, you bet I do. The images in this book are a combination of behind the scenes photographs and special moments from the beginning of Training Camp all the way to the Ring Ceremony.

They say a picture is worth a thousand words. While I was photographing the crowd from the top of Mr. Benson's float during the Victory Parade, I saw a young girl with a sign that said,

"Thank You Because It's So Much More Than Football"

This is truly how the New Orleans Saints Organization feels about the Gulf Coast Region and our Fans.

A man once told me that the Birth of the Saints did more to bring the people of New Orleans together than its Cuisine or Music. And as the years passed, the Saints not only pulled the people of the City of New Orleans together, but also joined an entire region together. The man who came up with this theory is known to Saints fans as Buddy D. I had the opportunity to work with Buddy Diliberto on the book titled *"When The Saints Came Marching In"* after the 2000 season when the team had won their first Playoff Game in Franchise History. According to Buddy D, the first big book project for Saints fans was titled "The Saga of the Saints" by Wayne Mack which reviewed the first 25 seasons of the franchise and that the third Saints book should not be published until the Saints won the Super Bowl. "THREE would be the Charm," he said. Bobby granted Buddy D's first wish and wore the dress, and now for the Charm, it's the Third Book..

"The Official Behind The Scenes Perspective of The Super Bowl XLIV Champion New Orleans Saints."

This book includes many exclusive images: the Saints' Private Ring Ceremony held at the Roosevelt Hotel when the entire organization was awarded Super Bowl Rings made by Tiffany & Company; Head Coach Sean Payton sleeping on the plane ride home from Miami with the Lombardi Trophy in his lap; Drew Brees and the offensive team practicing in a ballroom at our team hotel behind closed doors during the week of the Super Bowl; and the World Champions private concert performance by country music Superstar Kenny Chesney after the game.

Jim and Hokie made their now famous radio call that Pigs have flown after our win against the Vikings for the NFC Championship in the Superdome, and yes, we actually have a photograph of a pig flying at our Victory Parade in the streets of New Orleans.

A special feature about this book is that the photographs do not have captions. Instead, people inside the Saints organization included their own personal quotes to describe how they felt about a particular photograph. One of my favorite quotes came from Deuce McAllister as he described his feelings about being one of the Captains for the Playoff game against the Cardinals.

"Men are taught that they are not supposed to cry. Whoever said that didn't get the honor of leading their teammates onto the field in the Superdome in front of the best fans in the National Football League like I did. It's OK to Cry."

To Mr. Tom Benson and the Entire Saints Organization, thanks for allowing me to share the private moments of our team from behind the scenes. Your trust means everything to me. To Bennett's Camera the Official Photographic Supplier of the New Orleans Saints, thanks for everything you do for us Chris. To my brother and long-time assistant Steve, thanks for having my back. To Kim, Brittany, and Brad, thanks for sharing the dream.

We are World Champions!

New Orleans native Michael C. Hebert serves as director of photography for the World Champion New Orleans Saints. He is a graduate of Archbishop Rummel High School and Tulane University.

Michael C. Hebert
Director of Photography

Executive Editor:
Rita Benson LeBlanc

Photography & Editor:
Michael C. Hebert,
Director of Photography – Saints

Design & Production:
National Communications Group, Inc.
Scott May, President
Rob Krolick, Vice President
Jay Baumann, Designer

Printed in Canada

SAINTS 31 SAINTS 31 COLTS 1

SUPER BOWL XLIV